# MEDIA AND INFORMATION LITERACY IN HIGHER EDUCATION

CHANDOS
INFORMATION PROFESSIONAL SERIES
Series Editor: Ruth Rikowski
(email: Rikowskigr@aol.com)

Chandos' new series of books is aimed at the busy information professional. They have been specially commissioned to provide the reader with an authoritative view of current thinking. They are designed to provide easy-to-read and (most importantly) practical coverage of topics that are of interest to librarians and other information professionals. If you would like a full listing of current and forthcoming titles, please visit www.chandospublishing.com.

**New authors**: we are always pleased to receive ideas for new titles; if you would like to write a book for Chandos, please contact Dr Glyn Jones on g.jones.2@elsevier.com or telephone +44 (0) 1865 843000.

# MEDIA AND INFORMATION LITERACY IN HIGHER EDUCATION
## Educating the Educators

Edited by

**Siri Ingvaldsen**

**Dianne Oberg**

AMSTERDAM • BOSTON • HEIDELBERG • LONDON
NEW YORK • OXFORD • PARIS • SAN DIEGO
SAN FRANCISCO • SINGAPORE • SYDNEY • TOKYO
Chandos Publishing is an imprint of Elsevier

Chandos Publishing is an imprint of Elsevier
50 Hampshire Street, 5th Floor, Cambridge, MA 02139, United States
The Boulevard, Langford Lane, Kidlington, OX5 1GB, United Kingdom

Copyright © 2017 Elsevier Ltd. All rights reserved.

No part of this publication may be reproduced or transmitted in any form or by any means, electronic or mechanical, including photocopying, recording, or any information storage and retrieval system, without permission in writing from the publisher. Details on how to seek permission, further information about the Publisher's permissions policies and our arrangements with organizations such as the Copyright Clearance Center and the Copyright Licensing Agency, can be found at our website: www.elsevier.com/permissions.

This book and the individual contributions contained in it are protected under copyright by the Publisher (other than as may be noted herein).

**Notices**
Knowledge and best practice in this field are constantly changing. As new research and experience broaden our understanding, changes in research methods, professional practices, or medical treatment may become necessary.

Practitioners and researchers must always rely on their own experience and knowledge in evaluating and using any information, methods, compounds, or experiments described herein. In using such information or methods they should be mindful of their own safety and the safety of others, including parties for whom they have a professional responsibility.

To the fullest extent of the law, neither the Publisher nor the authors, contributors, or editors, assume any liability for any injury and/or damage to persons or property as a matter of products liability, negligence or otherwise, or from any use or operation of any methods, products, instructions, or ideas contained in the material herein.

**British Library Cataloguing-in-Publication Data**
A catalogue record for this book is available from the British Library

**Library of Congress Cataloging-in-Publication Data**
A catalog record for this book is available from the Library of Congress

ISBN: 978-0-08-100630-6 (print)
ISBN: 978-0-08-100631-3 (online)

For information on all Chandos Publishing
visit our website at https://www.elsevier.com

  **Working together to grow libraries in developing countries**

www.elsevier.com • www.bookaid.org

*Publisher:* Glyn Jones
*Acquisition Editor:* George Knott
*Editorial Project Manager:* Tessa de Roo
*Production Project Manager:* Debasish Ghosh
*Cover Designer:* Greg Harris

Typeset by MPS Limited, Chennai, India
**Transferred to Digital Printing in 2017**

# CONTENTS

*List of Contributors*     *ix*
*About the Authors*     *xi*
*Preface*     *xv*

**Chapter 1**    **Convergences of and for Media and Information Literacy Instruction in Higher Education**     **1**
D. Oberg
    1.1 Introduction     1
    1.2 MIL Instruction in School Libraries     2
    1.3 MIL Instruction in Academic Libraries     5
    1.4 Conclusion     10
    References     11

**Chapter 2**    **Teaching the Ethical Use of Information as an MIL Skill**     **13**
B. Schultz-Jones
    2.1 Introduction     13
    2.2 Ethics     13
    2.3 Information Literacy     14
    2.4 Placing Ethics in Information Literacy Competences     17
    2.5 Ethical Principles for Information Literacy     20
    2.6 Learning Environment     24
    2.7 Teaching Ethics as a MIL Skill     25
    2.8 Integrating Ethics in Teaching Information Literacy     31
    2.9 Conclusion     33
    References     34

**Chapter 3**    **Promoting Civic Literacy in Teacher Education: A Framework for Personal and Professional Development**     **37**
K. Flornes
    3.1 Introduction     37
    3.2 Media and Information Literacy and Human Rights     38
    3.3 Teacher Education in Norway     40
    3.4 Educating the Information-Literate Teacher: A Pilot Project     41
    3.5 The Construction of an MIL Approach in Teacher Education     44

|  |  |  |
|---|---|---|
|  | 3.6 Religious Education and MIL | 45 |
|  | 3.7 Conclusion | 48 |
|  | References | 49 |
| **Chapter 4** | **The School Library in Media and Information Literacy Education** | **51** |
|  | S. Ingvaldsen |  |
|  | 4.1 Introduction | 51 |
|  | 4.2 Media and Information Literacy: A Complex Set of Skills | 52 |
|  | 4.3 Teaching Media and Information Literacy | 53 |
|  | 4.4 Collaboration and Anchoring | 57 |
|  | 4.5 Learning Environments and Resources | 61 |
|  | 4.6 Integrating the Use of Libraries in Pedagogical Work | 62 |
|  | 4.7 Concluding Remarks | 63 |
|  | References | 64 |
| **Chapter 5** | **Teaching Faculty Collaborating With Academic Librarians: Developing Partnerships to Embed Information Literacy** | **67** |
|  | T. Inzerilla |  |
|  | 5.1 Introduction | 67 |
|  | 5.2 Faculty Collaborating With Librarians | 68 |
|  | 5.3 Methodology | 70 |
|  | 5.4 Faculty's Experience of Collaboration | 73 |
|  | 5.5 Motivating Factors and Challenges of Collaboration | 76 |
|  | 5.6 Ways Librarians Can Become Embedded in Faculty's Class Instruction | 80 |
|  | 5.7 Recommendations for Practice | 83 |
|  | 5.8 Conclusion | 84 |
|  | Acknowledgments | 86 |
|  | References | 86 |
| **Chapter 6** | **Teaching Source Criticism to Students in Higher Education: A Practical Approach** | **89** |
|  | H. Johannessen |  |
|  | 6.1 Introduction | 89 |
|  | 6.2 Information Literacy and Different Learning Theories | 89 |
|  | 6.3 One-Shot Instruction, Subject-Specific Adjustments, and Media and Information Literacy | 93 |
|  | 6.4 Teaching Source Criticism as Part of Information Literacy: When Does One Start to Evaluate? | 94 |

|  |  |  |
|---|---|---|
| 6.5 | Teaching Students to Search for and Assess Sources | 95 |
| 6.6 | The Five Ws Approach to Source Criticism: Evaluating Sources and Assessing Search Results | 96 |
| 6.7 | Using the Five Ws in Library Instruction | 98 |
| 6.8 | The Citation Compass: Source Criticism Online | 98 |
| 6.9 | Academic Texts | 100 |
| 6.10 | The Internet as a Source for Information | 101 |
| 6.11 | Evaluating Nonacademic Sources and Identifying Their Source Value | 101 |
| 6.12 | Teaching Complex Skills in One-Shot Instruction | 102 |
| 6.13 | Source Consciousness | 102 |
| 6.14 | Conclusions | 103 |
| References | | 104 |

### Chapter 7  Staff Development Programs on Teaching Skills and Curriculum Integration of Academic and Information Literacy at the University of Auckland — 107

L. Wang and S. Cook

|  |  |  |
|---|---|---|
| 7.1 | Introduction | 107 |
| 7.2 | The University of Auckland Libraries Learning Services | 108 |
| 7.3 | Presenter Training Program | 109 |
| 7.4 | Curriculum Integration of Academic and Information Literacy Program | 112 |
| 7.5 | Conclusion | 116 |
| References | | 117 |

### Chapter 8  IMPACT Lessons: Strategically Embedding Media and Information Literacy Through Teacher Development in Higher Education — 119

M. Flierl, C. Maybee, C.F. Riehle and N. Johnson

|  |  |  |
|---|---|---|
| 8.1 | Introduction | 119 |
| 8.2 | Teacher Development Initiatives: A MIL Opportunity | 120 |
| 8.3 | Librarians as Information Consultants | 123 |
| 8.4 | Opportunities for MIL Through Instructional Design | 124 |
| 8.5 | Embedding MIL Through Consultation: IMPACT Librarian Reflections | 127 |
| 8.6 | Conclusion | 132 |
| References | | 132 |

## Chapter 9  Action Research and Informed Learning for Transformative Professional Development About Information Literacy    **135**

A. Whisken

| | | |
|---|---|---|
| **9.1** | Introduction | 135 |
| **9.2** | Informed Learning and Information Literacy | 136 |
| **9.3** | Research Questions | 138 |
| **9.4** | Methodology | 138 |
| **9.5** | Context and Participation | 138 |
| **9.6** | Action Research Project | 139 |
| **9.7** | Findings | 140 |
| **9.8** | Summary of Findings | 148 |
| **9.9** | Implications for Practice | 149 |
| References | | 150 |

*Afterword*  *151*
*Index*  *153*

# LIST OF CONTRIBUTORS

**S. Cook**
University of Auckland, Auckland, New Zealand

**M. Flierl**
Purdue University, West Lafayette, IN, United States

**K. Flornes**
Bergen University College, Bergen, Norway

**S. Ingvaldsen**
Sogn og Fjordane County Library, Sogn og Fjordane, Norway

**T. Inzerilla**
Las Positas College Library, Livermore, CA, United States

**H. Johannessen**
Agder University Library, Bergen, Norway

**N. Johnson**
Purdue University, West Lafayette, IN, United States

**C. Maybee**
Purdue University, West Lafayette, IN, United States

**D. Oberg**
University of Alberta, Edmonton, AB, Canada

**C.F. Riehle**
Purdue University, West Lafayette, IN, United States

**B. Schultz-Jones**
University of North Texas, Denton, TX, United States

**L. Wang**
University of Auckland, Auckland, New Zealand

**A. Whisken**
Carey Baptist Grammar School, Kew, VIC, Australia

# ABOUT THE AUTHORS

**Christine Bruce** is Professor in the Information Systems School, Science and Engineering Faculty, Queensland University of Technology (QUT), Australia. She has an extensive research and publication profile in information research and learning, with special emphasis on information literacy and using information to learn in formal and informal learning environments. Her recent book publications on information literacy include *Informed Learning* (2008) and *Information Experience: Approaches to Theory and Practice* (2014). Christine regularly consults and facilitates workshops on information literacy in the university sector around the world.

**Stephanie Cook** (ORCID: 0000-0002-0308-8998) is a Learning Support Services Librarian at The University of Auckland Libraries and Learning Services, Auckland, New Zealand. She has over 20 years' experience in libraries and has coauthored several conference papers in the field of information literacy, student-centered learning approaches, and eLearning. In her current role she coordinates the Library's generic information literacy program, including organizing the Presenter Training program.

**Michael Flierl** is Assistant Professor and Learning Design Specialist at Purdue University Libraries, where he develops and leads the Libraries' efforts to empower diverse learners, including first-year, underrepresented minority, and international students, to use information critically to learn.

**Kari Flornes** is an Associate Professor in Religious Education at Bergen University College. She holds a PhD from the University of Birmingham (UK), based on her doctoral dissertation, *An Action Research Approach to Initial Teacher Education in Norway* (2007). She is also engaged in the Pestalozzi program in the Council of Europe and is the Vice President of the European NGO GERFEC (www.gerfec.eu).

**Catherine Fraser Riehle** is Associate Professor and Instructional Outreach Librarian at Purdue University Libraries where she serves as liaison for departments in the social sciences, and consults on, develops, and delivers a wide variety of instructional opportunities to engage students in research, critical thinking, and knowledge creation.

**Siri Ingvaldsen** was the Project Manager of the Norwegian School Library Program 2009–13, and Assistant Professor at the University of Agder, and UiT, the Arctic University of Norway. She has been involved in various research and development projects connected to the promotion of media and information literacy and reading education. Her main interest is the use of school libraries in the construction of children's learning. Ingvaldsen is now Head of Sogn og Fjordane County Library in Western Norway.

**Tina Inzerilla** is the Library Coordinator and a reference/instruction librarian at Las Positas College, a community college in California. She earned her PhD at Queensland University of Technology, Australia. Inzerilla enjoys collaborating with teaching faculty to incorporate information literacy into their courses.

**Hilde Johannessen** (Orchid: 0000-0002-1272-8731) is the head of Teaching and Research services at Agder University Library and liaison librarian for the Departments of Religion, Philosophy and History and Sociology and Social Work. She is currently the working group manager for The Norwegian Association of Higher Education's research support group. Her work is concentrated on library instruction, research support, and knowledge management. She was the project manager for the website *The Citation Compass* (2010–16). She holds a master's degree in religious studies and a bachelor's degree in literature. She coauthored the book *New Roles for Research Librarians: Meeting the Expectations for Research Support* (Chandos, 2016).

**Nastasha E. Johnson** is an Assistant Professor of Library Science and liaison to the Mathematics, Statistics, and Physics Departments. Her research interests include embedded information literacy and assessment. She joined Purdue University in 2013, from NC A&T State University, where she was an Assistant Professor and Reference & Instruction Librarian.

**Clarence Maybee** is Assistant Professor and Information Literacy Specialist in the Purdue University Libraries, where his work focuses on enabling student learning through information literacy. Maybee coordinates the Libraries' involvement in a teacher development program. He has presented and published regularly about his research exploring information literacy in higher education.

**Dianne Oberg** is a Professor Emerita in teacher-librarianship at the University of Alberta in Canada. Her research focuses on the education of teacher-librarians and the implementation and evaluation of school library programs. She coauthored with J. Branch the award-winning professional document *Focus on Inquiry: A Teacher's Guide to Implementing Inquiry-based Learning* (2004). She was the founding editor of the peer-reviewed journal, *School Libraries Worldwide*.

**Barbara Schultz-Jones** is an Associate Professor and Director of the School Library Program at the University of North Texas, Denton, Texas. Dr. Schultz-Jones served on the IFLA School Libraries Section, as Secretary 2011–13 and Chair 2013–15, coediting the IFLA *School Library Guidelines* (2nd edition) with Dianne Oberg. Her research focuses on school library learning environments.

**Li Wang** (ORCID: 0000-0002-2596-6827) is the Learning Support Services Manager at The University of Auckland Libraries and Learning Services, Auckland, New Zealand. She has been working in the area of information literacy education and eLearning since the 1990s, as a higher educator, a library practitioner, and a researcher. She is the author of many published articles and conference papers in the areas of information literacy, learning theories and practice, student-centered approach, and new technology used in information literacy education and eLearning design.

**Anne Whisken** is the Head of Resource Centre at Carey Baptist Grammar School, Melbourne, Australia. She has managed secondary school libraries in rapidly changing educational environments over four decades. A PhD candidate at Charles Sturt University, her action research project with teachers investigated use of Christine Bruce's *Informed Learning* models to bridge the gap between information literacy theory and practice.

# PREFACE

Media and information literacy (MIL) is increasingly a concept that matters. It is about issues that matter—about health, homelessness, abuse, disasters, migration, as well as about broad socioeconomic benefit. MIL is now widely recognized in policy and practice by governments, education departments, leading world agencies such as UNESCO, libraries, and other information agencies. MIL education is also recognized by many as a professional responsibility. In this climate, understanding what matters in bringing about MIL is crucial; and understanding what matters in bringing about MIL is also central to the purpose of educating the educators who are charged with that professional responsibility.

Empowering others to bring about MIL, deliberately diffusing strategies that work, is a key to bringing about the information-literate society so desperately needed in our digital age. When we consider the possibilities of diffusing innovations associated with educating the educators we start to develop a picture of what it takes to make possible empowering MIL experiences in many spaces: in formal and informal environments, in face-to-face and virtual learning spaces, in workplace, academic and community contexts. Profiling existing innovations for educating educators in one very special context—the higher education sector—is a core purpose of this book.

All the chapters represent contemporary advances in research, practice, or both. They are underpinned by a wide range of theoretical developments, and at the same time have a clear pragmatic purpose. Many are examples of orientation towards evidence-based practice in the field. The authors are deeply interested in learning theories and frameworks. Key ideas such as threshold concepts, inquiry, and informed learning are highlighted. In the chapters that follow, the authors explore the value that sociocultural approaches, social network analysis, and action research can play in building programs and insights important to "educating the educator." The role of the discipline, the curriculum, the community, and the library all play a part in constituting the environment to be considered.

Overall, powerful educational experiences rest on communication within educational teams, whether those be at colleges and universities, in schools or even our preschool environments, as well as the wider community and workplace context. We continue to need to understand that colleagues working together do not always share the same view of teaching, learning, or indeed of information literacy. As a consequence they do not always share the same understanding of desired learning outcomes or assessment processes. Overcoming these challenges is always critical in moving forward in any learning design process.

What about my own take on this? Educating the educators has always been a topic dear to my heart. I have always been interested in what information literacy is all about and how it is learned, particularly in terms of how it is experienced by others. People's experiences of information literacy continue to grow and develop. We know that while there are ways of talking about information literacy concepts, constructs, and experiences at a relatively high level of abstraction, to be meaningful these must be contextualized, and our insights into those experiences in different contexts continue to grow. The shape of people's vision of information literacy molds their practice. As visions of information literacy have transformed over the years, whilst remaining true to the original interpretation of information empowering lifelong learning in many contexts, so the chapters in this book reflect these transformations.

Educating the educators in higher education embraces educating the owners, designers, implementers, and supporters of a wide variety of educational environments and programs. It involves educating information professionals and teachers in their initial education. It involves professional development for many groups. Educating the educators embraces information professionals participating in professional development programs for educators, as well as leading segments of those programs. It involves staying abreast not only in developments associated with information literacy, but also in relation to learning technologies, learning theories, and discipline-based developments. It involves participating in, and leading others in, what is known as the scholarship of learning and teaching.

I commend to you the many innovations, representing both research and practice profiled in the following chapters. Each offers a unique lens on the current landscape associated with educating the educators for MIL leadership in higher education.

**C. Bruce**

# CHAPTER 1

# Convergences of and for Media and Information Literacy Instruction in Higher Education

**D. Oberg**
University of Alberta, Edmonton, AB, Canada

## 1.1 INTRODUCTION

The filing on February 2, 2015 of the *Framework for Information Literacy in Higher Education* by the Board of Directors of the American College and Research Libraries (ACRL) section of the American Library Association signaled some convergences in conceptions of media and information literacy (MIL). Two groups within the library sector traditionally have been committed to MIL instruction—school librarians and academic librarians—but in the past their theoretical and practical approaches to this work to a large extent have been quite different, and the developments in each field have been largely invisible to the other sector.

This chapter presents several approaches to MIL instruction: from school libraries, the process approach exemplified by Guided Inquiry (Kuhlthau, Maniotes, & Caspari, 2007, 2012) and from academic libraries, Informed Learning (Bruce, 2008) and the Framework for Information Literacy in Higher Education (ACRL, 2015). Several convergences between these approaches offer opportunities for "educators of educators"—school librarians, academic librarians, K-12 teachers, college and university teachers, and educators of teachers and of librarians—to draw upon and perhaps align their practices with the best in the theories and practices of both sectors.

Practitioners in both sectors of education have much to learn from each other, and the work of practitioners in each sector affects the work in the other sector. My special concern over a long career has been the education of teachers and school librarians, preparing them for their work with children and youth in K-12 schools. Academic librarians have been my partners in this endeavor, and my research on how teachers use libraries in their teaching has shown that they were influenced by their experiences with university librarians during their preservice teacher education (Oberg, 1993).

The concept of "educators of educators" in the title and content of this book reflects the awareness that MIL instruction can be initiated in many different ways, by individuals and by groups, carrying out many different roles in teaching and learning. Most often, the phrase "educators of educators" brings to mind university faculty members responsible for preparing university students for professional practice as teachers and librarians, but in the area of MIL education, this is not always the case. For example, students in a college class experiencing difficulty with the library searches necessary for completing an assignment might ask for help from their instructor who then accesses help for the class from the library staff. School librarians often provide informal professional development in MIL for their school leadership staff as part of initiating a whole-school approach to curriculum-integrated MIL instruction (Oberg, 2009). University faculty may reach out to academic librarians to discuss making improvements to a course assignment (Shorten, Wallace, & Crookes, 2001). College accrediting bodies may require that colleges give evidence of student achievement of information literacy outcomes in the college curriculum, which brings academic librarians and teaching faculty together to revise, implement, and evaluate information literacy-based curricula (Thompson, 2002).

## 1.2 MIL INSTRUCTION IN SCHOOL LIBRARIES

What is regarded as exemplary MIL instruction in school libraries has changed over the years: a source approach, during the 1960s and 1970s; a pathfinder approach, through the 1980s; and a process approach, beginning in the 1990s. The process approach has been implemented over the past 25 years under many different "labels" in the school libraries field; information literacy, MIL, inquiry-based instruction, and Guided Inquiry are just a few.

The process approach to teaching MIL emphasizes thinking about information and using information within a problem-solving perspective. It does not discard the knowledge from earlier approaches, such as the knowledge of tools, sources, and search strategies, but it does emphasize that this knowledge is to be developed within the teaching of thinking and problem-solving (Oberg, 1999, 2004).

The process approach is theory-based and grounded in research from the fields of education and of library and information studies (LIS). From education comes learning theory, and from LIS, information seeking behavior theory. For example, from education comes the knowledge that learners vary in the level of abstraction that they can handle, depending on their cognitive development and their prior knowledge and experience. Also from education come the constructivist concepts of learners actively building or constructing their knowledge and of learners experiencing changes in feelings as well as changes of thoughts as they use information. From LIS comes the knowledge that users of information progress through levels of question specificity, from vague notions of information need, to clearly defined needs or questions, and that users are more successful in the search process if they have a realistic understanding of the information system and of the information problem. From both education and LIS comes the understanding that students learn more about MIL when MIL instruction is connected to and integrated with disciplinary content and assignments.

The work on MIL instruction in the school libraries sector has been strongly influenced by the seminal research of Carol C. Kuhlthau whose doctoral work investigated the experiences of high school seniors completing library-based research assignments. Kuhlthau brought to her research a deep understanding of student learning, beginning from her early career as a kindergarten teacher and a school librarian. Kuhlthau's Model of the Information Search Process showed the affective, cognitive, and physical changes that learners experience as they complete a research project from task initiation to presentation. The process approach to inquiry goes beyond the location of information to the use of information, beyond the answering of a specific question to the seeking of evidence to shape a topic. It considers the process of a search for information as well as the product of the search. It calls for an awareness of the complexity of learning from information: learning from information is not a routine or standardized task, and it involves the affective as well as the cognitive domains. Throughout the process, learners benefit from support in dealing with the feelings, thoughts, and actions that are part of their information search process.

The goal of instruction is "to instill in students a sense of the process of learning from a variety of sources of information" (Kuhlthau, 1995, p. 1). This is true for college and university students as well as K-12 students; it is also true for professionals who engage in information use for solving problems—see, e.g., research into the use of information by financial analysts and judges (Kuhlthau, 2003). By providing opportunities for information users, whatever their age and stage of life, for reflecting on their feelings, thoughts, and actions throughout the process of learning through the use of information, information users develop an awareness and understanding of their own personal learning experience as well as an awareness and understanding of their new content knowledge. This metacognitive aspect of the process approach to MIL is critical to developing abilities related to self-directed learning, lifelong and life-wide.

## 1.2.1 Instructional Models in the K-12 School Library Sector

Kuhlthau's Model of the Information Search Process is the basis of the Guided Inquiry Model (Kuhlthau et al., 2007). Guided Inquiry is a model to guide MIL instruction in K-12 schools; the model is based on six principles:
- Children learn by being actively engaged in and reflecting on experience.
- Children learn by building on what they already know.
- Children develop higher-order thinking skills through guidance at critical points in the learning process.
- Children have different ways and modes of learning.
- Children learn through social interaction with others.
- Children learn through instruction and experience in accord with their cognitive development (Kuhlthau et al., 2007, p. 25).

Guided Inquiry offers a process model for teaching content and information use in an integrated and meaningful way (Table 1.1).

Instructional models support teachers and librarians in providing opportunities to develop students' metacognitive abilities. As demonstrated in the *Focus on Inquiry* model (Alberta Learning, 2004), developed

**Table 1.1** Phases of the Guided Inquiry process (summary)

| | |
|---|---|
| Open | Invitation to inquiry, open minds, stimulate curiosity |
| Immerse | Build background knowledge, connect to content, discover interesting ideas |
| Explore | Explore interesting ideas, look around, dip in |
| Identify | Pause and ponder, identify an inquiry question, decide direction |
| Gather | Gather important information, go broad, go deep |
| Create | Reflect on learning, go beyond facts to make meaning, create to communicate |
| Share | Learn from each other, share learning, tell your story |
| Evaluate | Evaluate achievement of learning goals, reflect on content, reflect on process |

Kuhlthau et al. (2012, pp. 1−6).

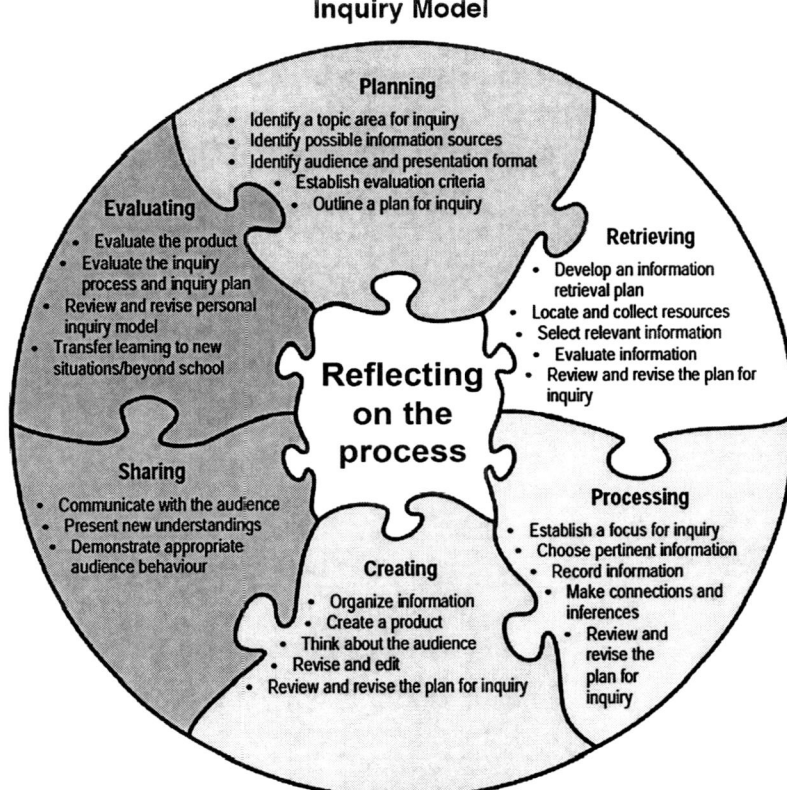

Figure 1.1 Focus on Inquiry Model (Alberta Learning, 2004, p. 10).

in Alberta, Canada, reflecting on the process is critical throughout the process for developing metacognitive understandings and strategies (http://open.alberta.ca/publications/0778526666) (Fig. 1.1).

## 1.3 MIL INSTRUCTION IN ACADEMIC LIBRARIES

In academic libraries, MIL instruction is offered under many terms; bibliographic instruction, library instruction, information literacy, and informed learning are a few.

What is regarded as exemplary MIL instruction in academic libraries has changed over the years: however, the requirement of one-shot instructional models continues as a challenge in many academic library settings. Current approaches to MIL instruction in academic libraries are exemplified by the *Framework for Information Literacy in Higher Education* (ACRL, 2015) and *Informed Learning* (Bruce, 2008).

### 1.3.1 Framework for Information Literacy in Higher Education

In North America, academic librarians and their partners in higher education have been looking for new approaches to enhance their longstanding guidelines for MIL instruction, the *Information Literacy Competency Standards for Higher Education* (ACRL, 2000). As noted by Johannessen in her chapter about source criticism, the 2000 *Standards* are based on a behavioristic view of information literacy which emphasizes measurable skills that are not subject-specific, but generic and transferrable. According to the 2000 *Standards*, the information-literate student:

- Determines the nature and extent of information needed;
- Accesses needed information effectively and efficiently;
- Evaluates information and its sources critically and incorporates selected information into his or her knowledge base and value system;
- Individually or as a member of a group, uses information effectively to accomplish a specific purpose;
- Understands many of the economic, legal, and social issues surrounding the use of information, and accesses and uses information ethically and legally (ACRL, 2000, pp. 8–14).

Each of these five competencies has a number of performance indicators (22 in all) or measurable learning outcomes.

ACRL has recommended that the 2000 *Standards* be sunsetted (removed from active use) by July 1, 2016, in favor of the new *Framework*. The 2015 ACRL *Framework for Information Literacy in Higher Education*, is built around six core concepts, or frames:

- Authority is constructed and contextual;
- Information creation as a process;
- Information has value;
- Research as inquiry;
- Scholarship as conversation; and
- Searching as strategic exploration.

Each core concept is illustrated through knowledge practices and dispositions. Knowledge practices are ways in which learners can demonstrate their understanding and use of the core concepts, or frames, while dispositions are related to the attitudes and values that underpin the core concepts. For example, one of the frames, Searching as Strategic Exploration, states that: "Searching for information is often nonlinear and iterative, requiring the evaluation of a range of information sources and the mental flexibility to pursue alternate avenues as new understanding develops." Learners who are developing their information literate abilities "utilize divergent (e.g., brainstorming) and convergent (e.g., selecting the best source) thinking when searching" (a knowledge practice) and "exhibit mental flexibility and creativity" (a disposition) (ACRL, 2015, p. 9).

As Carncross (2015) notes, the implementation of the *Framework* requires a shift in the focus of instruction from skills to process. This is well illustrated by comparing the definitions of information literacy of the *Standards* and the *Framework*:

> Information literacy is a set of abilities requiring individuals to recognize when information is needed and have the ability to locate, evaluate and use effectively the needed information.
>
> *ACRL (2000, p. 2)*

> Information literacy is the set of integrated abilities encompassing the reflective discovery of information, the understanding of how information is produced and valued, and the use of information in creating new knowledge and participating ethically in communities of learning.
>
> *ACRL (2015, p. 3)*

It is not expected that the frames or core concepts be taught as stand-alone skills or that they be taught in a specified order. Instead, it is expected that these core concepts of MIL are developed as part of an integrated approach to instruction, as part of disciplinary or content learning, not taught in isolation from content.

### 1.3.2 Informed Learning

Informed Learning is "using information, creatively and effectively in order to learn" (Bruce, 2008, p. viii). The idea of Informed Learning builds upon Bruce's early research with university faculty in Australia from which emerged "seven faces of information literacy" (Bruce, 1997). Informed Learning is the kind of learning made possible through evolving and transferable capacity to use information to learn in education, in the workplace, and in community settings.

Three principles underpin Informed Learning:
1. Informed Learning takes into account learners' experiences.
2. Informed Learning promotes the simultaneous development of discipline learning and process learning.

3. Informed Learning is about changes in experience (Bruce, 2008, pp. 12–13).

These principles shape the work of librarians and teachers in developing programs of media and information education. Not only must librarians and teachers be aware of students' learning experience, they must help their students be aware of their own learning experience. This means building relevant experiences into the curriculum, and ensuring that the students have opportunities to reflect on their experiences and to apply what they have learned to "novel contexts." Librarians and teachers need to create learning activities that allow students to experience both information use and subject content in an integrated way. Librarians and teachers need to help students see the world in new and complex ways as they develop new and complex ways of working with information. This means that school librarians and academic librarians need to collaborate with teaching faculty in developing programs of MIL education that are integrated with curriculum, with courses, and with programs.

The seven faces of Informed Learning describe the different ways that information use can be experienced and suggest different focuses or goals for learning design:
1. The information awareness and communication experience;
2. The sourcing information experience;
3. The information process experience;
4. The information control experience;
5. The knowledge construction experience;
6. The knowledge extension experience;
7. The wisdom experience.

The six frames of Informed Learning provide a conceptual framework for analyzing theoretical influences that shape teaching and learning related to MIL instruction: content; competency; learning to learn; personal relevance; social impact; and relational. Each frame or lens applies to a goal for learning about information and about subject content and includes a view of: information literacy; information; teaching and learning; curriculum focus; content; and assessment.

## 1.3.3 Convergences

Throughout this chapter and throughout this book, readers will recognize a number of convergences between these approaches for MIL education. Here is a starter's list of convergences.

### 1.3.3.1 A Process Approach

Current models guiding MIL instruction emphasize teaching the process, not standalone skills. The process of using information to learn is not linear, but highly individual, flexible, and more recursive than might be suggested in traditional models outlining how to use information for learning. Working from the core concepts or frames of the 2015 ACRL *Framework* will suggest important shifts that need to be made in the conceptualization and practice of MIL education. The frames resonate strongly with those in the school library field. Twenty years ago, school library researcher Ross Todd laid out five principles of effective information literacy instruction:
1. Instruction is a conversation.
2. Effective teaching of information literacy consists of four essential component processes: discursive, adaptive, interactive, and reflective.
3. Action without useable feedback is not productive for the learner.
4. The design of information literacy programs should be open.
5. Establishing an effective learning environment is critical to successful information literacy instruction. (Todd, 1995a, pp. 65–67)

### 1.3.3.2 An Integrated Approach

Current models of MIL instruction involve the simultaneous consideration of information use and disciplinary content. Research has shown the power of teaching skills and concepts within a meaningful context, within courses and across programs (see, e.g., Klinger, Lee, Stephenson, Deluca, & Luu, 2009; Shorten et al., 2001; Thompson, 2002; Todd, 1995b). For starting points in the design of curriculum-integrated information use activities, school librarians can turn to the plethora of curriculum documents provided to educators in K-12 schools; academic librarians, on the other hand, must generally turn to their teaching faculty for that information. Here is where the one-shot approach to MIL instruction entrenched in many institutions presents difficult challenges: skills taught in isolation from meaningful disciplinary content are soon forgotten.

### 1.3.3.3 A Collaborative Approach

Librarians and teachers bring different expertise to MIL education. Collaboration is critical but often difficult to explain and implement. Montiel-Overall (2005) proposes four models or levels of TLC, or teacher and librarian collaboration: A, coordination; B, cooperation; C, integrated instruction; and D, integrated curriculum. The levels of collaboration, from A to D, appear to have increasing potential for positively affecting learning, especially where there is attention paid to: (1) interest; (2) level of involvement; (3) improved learning; (4) innovation; and (5) integration in teacher and librarian collaboration. Finding a place to start with collaboration is often difficult. Here Bruce's *Informed Learning* text offers conceptual frames for identifying the views that librarians and teachers bring to the learning design table.

### 1.3.3.4 Attending to the Learner's Experience
Learning design needs to start with awareness of students' background knowledge and experience. This includes drawing from research about the feelings, thoughts, and actions experienced by individuals involved in inquiry activities. Here Kuhlthau's 2003 *Seeking Meaning* text is an invaluable resource, for providing vivid descriptions of the phenomenon of inquiry as well as for providing practical advice and strategies for interventions in the difficult stages of the inquiry process.

### 1.3.3.5 Supporting Metacognition and Reflection
Learning design needs to consider the importance of the learners' or inquirers' thinking about their personal learning processes. At all levels of education, students should be given opportunities to understand that inquiry is a personal and highly individual learning process. Reflecting on their process in writing or in conversation with others (peers, faculty, librarians) will help students to develop their metacognitive skills—thinking about their thinking and thinking about their feelings—and to develop strategies for monitoring and enhancing their personal learning process.

## 1.4 CONCLUSION

For "educators of educators"—school librarians, academic librarians, K-12 teachers, college and university teachers, and educators of teachers and of librarians—these convergences invite exploration of the foundational theories and best practices of both the school library sector and the academic library sector. As noted earlier, practitioners in both sectors of education have much to learn from each other, and the work of practitioners in either sector affects the work in the other sector.

Academic librarians in colleges and universities are being expected to work in collaboration with teaching faculty in ways that have long been the expectation for librarians and teachers in K-12 schools. In colleges and universities, academic librarians face many challenges in developing programs of MIL instruction (Julien, 2005), including "prescriptive guidelines which encourage a surface learning approach; delivery by librarians who may lack both educational training and power to influence the curriculum; and poor assessment methods" (Johnston & Webber, 2003, p. 335). School librarians often face similar challenges. We can and should learn from each other; sometimes we can even work together across institutional divides (Oakleaf & Owen, 2010)!

## REFERENCES

ACRL. (2000). Information literacy competency standards for higher education. Retreived from: http://www.ala.org/acrl/standards/informationliteracycompetency.

ACRL. (2015). Framework for information literacy in higher education. Retrieved from: http://www.ala.org/acrl/standards/ilframework.

Alberta Learning (2004). *Focus on inquiry: A teacher's guide to inquiry-based learning.* Edmonton, Canada: Alberta Learning, Learning Resources Branch.

Bruce, C. S. (1997). *Seven faces of information literacy.* Adelaide, Australia: AUSLIB Press.

Bruce, C. S. (2008). *Informed learning.* Chicago: Association of College and Research Libraries, A Division of the American Library Association.

Carncross, M. (2015). Redeveloping a course with the *Framework for Information Literacy for Higher Education*: From skills to process. *College & Research Libraries News, 5*(76), 248−250, 273.

Johnston, B., & Webber, S. (2003). Information literacy in higher education: A review and case study. *Studies in Higher Education, 28*(3), 335−352. Available from: http://dx.doi.org/10.1080/03075070309295.

Julien, H. (2005). Education for information literacy instruction: A global perspective. *Journal of Education for Library and Information Science, 46*(3), 210−216.

Klinger, D. A., Lee, E. A., Stephenson, G., Deluca, C., & Luu, K. (2009). *Exemplary school libraries in Ontario.* Toronto, Canada: Ontario Library Association.

Kuhlthau, C. C. (1995). The process of learning from information. *School Libraries Worldwide, 1*(1), 1−12.

Kuhlthau, C. C. (2003). *Seeking meaning: A process approach to library and information services* (2nd ed.). Westport, CT: Libraries Unlimited.

Kuhlthau, C. C., Maniotes, L. K., & Casperi, A. K. (2007). *Guided Inquiry: Learning in the 21st century.* Westport, CT: Libraries Unlimited.

Kuhlthau, C. C., Maniotes, L. K., & Casperi, A. K. (2012). *Guided Inquiry design: A framework for inquiry in your school.* Santa Barbara, CA: Libraries Unlimited.

Montiel-Overall, P. (2005). Toward a theoretical understanding of teacher and librarian collaboration (TLC). *School Libraries Worldwide, 11*(2), 24−48.

Oakleaf, M., & Owen, P. L. (2010). Closing the 12−13 gap together: School and college librarians supporting 21st century learners. *Teacher Librarian, 37*(4), 52−58.

Oberg, D. (1993). Use of libraries in teaching by novice and experienced teachers. *School Libraries in Canada, 13*(3), 14−19.

Oberg, D. (1999). Teaching the research process—For discovery and personal growth. In: Section of School Libraries and Resource Centers, conference proceedings of the 65th IFLA conference and general council, held in Bangkok, Thailand (Booklet 3, pp. 52−60). Available online: http://www.ifla.org/IV/ifla65/papers/078-119e.htm.

Oberg, D. (2004). Promoting information literacies: A focus on inquiry. In: Conference proceedings of the 70th IFLA general council and conference, section of School Libraries and Resource Centers, Buenos Aires, Argentina. Available online at: http://www.ifla.org/IV/ifla70/papers/088e-Oberg.pdf, 14 pp. Also available in translation (Spanish and French).

Oberg, D. (2009). Libraries in schools: Essential contexts for studying organizational change and culture. *Library Trends, 58*(1), 9–25.

Shorten, A., Wallace, C., & Crookes, P. A. (2001). Developing information literacy: A key to evidence-based nursing. *International Nursing Review, 48*, 86–92. Available from: http://dx.doi.org/10.1046/j.1466-7657.2001.00045.x.

Thompson, G. B. (2002). Information literacy accreditation mandates: What they mean for faculty and librarians. *Library Trends, 51*(2), 218–241.

Todd, R. J. (1995a). Information literacy: Philosophy, principles, and practice. *School Libraries Worldwide, 1*(1), 54–68.

Todd, R. J. (1995b). Integrated information skills instruction: Does it make a difference? *School Library Media Quarterly, 23*(2), 133–138.

# CHAPTER 2

# Teaching the Ethical Use of Information as an MIL Skill

B. Schultz-Jones
University of North Texas, Denton, TX, United States

## 2.1 INTRODUCTION

What do educators need to know about teaching the ethical use of information? This chapter deals with teaching the ethical use of information as a media and information literacy (MIL) skill. To be able to use information ethically, educators and students must equip themselves with principles that can be applied as information literacy skills to our information landscape. The concepts of ethics and information literacy are examined and the connection between the learning environment and the adoption of ethical information literacy skills is discussed. The teaching frameworks of informed learning (Bruce, 2008) and guided inquiry (Kuhlthau, Maniotes, & Caspari, 2012) are explored, along with learning scenarios, as a means of orchestrating the adoption of ethical information literacy behavior.

## 2.2 ETHICS

The term *ethics* occurs in many examples of standards and guidelines that address the acquisition, use, dissemination, and impact of information. The term is used as a simple way to highlight the recognition of right and wrong conduct in relation to handling information and as a more complex concept that identifies a principled approach to dealing with increasingly sophisticated information technology and its ever-changing global environment. As educators we have the opportunity to address the principles and standards needed to make wise decisions when dealing with the complexity of information issues of our 21st century. We recognize that the values of a community may vary across cultures. However, in a complex information environment, there are principles and values that we need to establish and reinforce. The educational community fosters engagement with these values in our learning environment and provides the means to learn and understand ethical information literacy behavior.

## 2.3 INFORMATION LITERACY

An appreciation of teaching the ethical use of information as a literacy skill begins with an appreciation of the evolution of information literacy. In the United States, the concept of information literacy has evolved from a simple definition that referred to the approach of using reference resources to find information, through a recognition by the Association of College and Research Libraries (ACRL) of the American Library Association (ALA, 1989) definition that being information-literate meant being equipped with a set of abilities requiring individuals to "recognize when information is needed and have the ability to locate, evaluate, and effectively use the needed information" (ACRL, 2000, p. 2), to a grouping of "threshold concepts" and "foundational ideas" that are intended to address the "dynamic and often uncertain information ecosystem in which all of us work and live" (ACRL, 2015, p. 2).

With the 2007 publication of *Standards for the 21st Century Learner* the American Association of School Librarians (AASL) recognized that the "definition of information literacy has become more complex as resources and technologies have changed" (p. 3) and highlighted that "multiple literacies, including digital, visual, textual, and technological, have now joined information as crucial skills for this century" (p. 3). An expanded definition of information literacy seeks to address a wider, more encompassing reach throughout a path of lifelong learning:

> *Information literacy is the set of integrated abilities encompassing the reflective discovery of information, the understanding of how information is produced and valued, and the use of information in creating new knowledge and participating ethically in communities of learning.*
>
> *ACRL (2015, p. 3)*

The Canadian Library Association (CLA, 2014) adopted *Standards of Practice for School Library Learning Commons in Canada* that articulate five core standards of practice to "drive best teaching and learning through the Library Learning Commons" (p. 8). The fourth standard, Fostering Literacies to Empower Life-Long Learners, applies an expanded "notion of literacy" that includes "digital literacy and citizenship" (pp. 17–18), recognizing that students must develop a range of literacy skills that includes personal responsibility. Accompanying the range of literacy skills is a continuum of growth indicators that identify the various competencies students would achieve throughout the various stages of exploring, emerging, evolving, and established.

The International Federation of Library Associations (IFLA, 2006) notes that there is a difference among languages in handling the concept of information literacy and the use of information *competency* is more easily recognized outside the English-speaking nations (p. 9). A recommendation by the European Council (2006) of the European Union identified eight key competences for lifelong learning (see Table 2.1).

These competences are recognized as "a combination of knowledge, skills and attitudes appropriate to the context. They are particularly necessary for personal fulfilment and development, social inclusion, active citizenship and employment" (European Council, 2006, Summary). Of the eight competences, competences four, five, six, and seven relate to the use of information. The acknowledgment of personal

Table 2.1 Key competences for lifelong learning

| Key competence | Essential knowledge, skills, and attitudes |
| --- | --- |
| Communication in the mother tongue | The ability to express and interpret concepts, thoughts, feelings, facts, and opinions in both oral and written form (listening, speaking, reading, and writing) and to interact linguistically in an appropriate and creative way in a full range of societal and cultural contexts |
| Communication in foreign languages | Involves, in addition to the main skill dimensions of communication in the mother tongue, mediation and intercultural understanding. The level of proficiency depends on several factors and the capacity for listening, speaking, reading, and writing |
| Mathematical competence and basic competences in science and technology | The ability to develop and apply mathematical thinking in order to solve a range of problems in everyday situations, with the emphasis being placed on process, activity, and knowledge. Basic competences in science and technology refer to the mastery, use, and application of knowledge and methodologies that explain the natural world. These involve an understanding of the changes caused by human activity and the responsibility of each individual as a citizen |

(*Continued*)

**Table 2.1** (Continued)

| Key competence | Essential knowledge, skills, and attitudes |
|---|---|
| Digital competence | The confident and critical use of information society technology and thus basic skills in information and communication technology |
| Learning to learn | Related to learning, the ability to pursue and organize one's own learning, either individually or in groups, in accordance with one's own needs, and awareness of methods and opportunities |
| Social and civic competences | Social competence refers to personal, interpersonal, and intercultural competence and all forms of behavior that equip individuals to participate in an effective and constructive way in social and working life. It is linked to personal and social well-being. An understanding of codes of conduct and customs in the different environments in which individuals operate is essential. Civic competence, and particularly knowledge of social and political concepts and structures (democracy, justice, equality, citizenship, and civil rights), equips individuals to engage in active and democratic participation |
| Sense of initiative and entrepreneurship | The ability to turn ideas into action. It involves creativity, innovation, and risk-taking, as well as the ability to plan and manage projects in order to achieve objectives. The individual is aware of the context of his/her work and is able to seize opportunities that arise. It is the foundation for acquiring more specific skills and knowledge needed by those establishing or contributing to social or commercial activity. This should include awareness of ethical values and promote good governance |
| Cultural awareness and expression | Appreciation of the importance of the creative expression of ideas, experiences, and emotions in a range of media (music, performing arts, literature, and the visual arts) |

Recommendation 2006/962/EC of the European Parliament and of the Council of Dec. 18, 2006.

responsibility and sensitivity to societal interactions is interwoven throughout all eight of these competences. The multifaceted nature of information competency is clearly demonstrated.

Underlying the use of definitions to describe information literacy and/or competence is the recognition that there is an ethical foundation to the use of information, both individually and as a society; there are consequences to how we handle information, both individually and as a society.

## 2.4 PLACING ETHICS IN INFORMATION LITERACY COMPETENCES

As a core competence for information literacy, ethics maintains a high profile. As one of the common beliefs in the AASL (2007) *Standards for the 21st Century Learner*:

> Ethical behaviour in the use of information must be taught. In this increasingly global world of information, students must be taught to seek diverse perspectives, gather and use information ethically, and use social tools responsibly and safely. (p. 2)

And again in the use of skills, resources, and tools, the idea that being a member of our democratic society requires ethical participation:

Learners use skills, resources, and tools to:
1. Inquire, think critically, and gain knowledge.
2. Draw conclusions, make informed decisions, apply knowledge to new situations, and create new knowledge.
3. Share knowledge and participate ethically and productively as members of our democratic society.
4. Pursue personal and esthetic growth. (AASL, 2007, p. 3).

In the ACRL (2000) *Information Literacy Competency Standards*, the ethical use of information was recognized as Standard Five (see Table 2.2).

With the broadened ACRL (2015) *Framework for Information Literacy* perspective, the ethical use of information resides within each of the seven foundational concepts (see Table 2.3).

With the background and transition of concepts established, let's combine the concepts as ethical information literacy behavior since literacy involves awareness to inform practice and the development of skills to apply practice. We will discuss what that means and how we can transfer these concepts to others, and build an ethical foundation for the use of information.

**Table 2.2** ACRL information literacy competency standard five (ACRL, 2000, p. 14)

| Performance indicators | Outcomes |
|---|---|
| 1. The information-literate student understands many of the ethical, legal and socio-economic issues surrounding information and information technology | a. Identifies and discusses issues related to privacy and security in both the print and electronic environments<br>b. Identifies and discusses issues related to free versus fee-based access to information<br>c. Identifies and discusses issues related to censorship and freedom of speech<br>d. Demonstrates an understanding of intellectual property, copyright, and fair use of copyrighted material |
| 2. The information-literate student follows laws, regulations, institutional policies, and etiquette related to the access and use of information resources | a. Participates in electronic discussions following accepted practices (eg, "Netiquette")<br>b. Uses approved passwords and other forms of ID for access to information resources<br>c. Complies with institutional policies on access to information resources<br>d. Preserves the integrity of information resources, equipment, systems, and facilities<br>e. Legally obtains, stores, and disseminates text, data, images, or sounds<br>f. Demonstrates an understanding of what constitutes plagiarism and does not represent work attributable to others as his/her own<br>g. Demonstrates an understanding of institutional policies related to human subjects research |
| 3. The information-literate student acknowledges the use of information sources in communicating the product or performance | a. Selects an appropriate documentation style and uses it consistently to cite sources<br>b. Posts permission-granted notices, as needed, for copyrighted material |

The information-literate student understands many of the economic, legal, and social issues surrounding the use of information and accesses and uses information ethically and legally.

**Table 2.3** Ethics extracts from ACRL (2015) framework for information literacy

| Knowledge practices | Dispositions |
|---|---|
| **Concept: authority is constructed and contextual** | |
| Learners who are developing their information-literate abilities:<br>• Acknowledge they are developing their own authoritative voices in a particular area and recognize the responsibilities this entails, including seeking accuracy and reliability, respecting intellectual property, and participating in communities of practice | Learners who are developing their information-literate abilities:<br>• Develop awareness of the importance of assessing content with a skeptical stance and with a self-awareness of their own biases and worldview |
| **Concept: information creation as a process** | |
| Learners who are developing their information-literate abilities:<br>• Develop, in their own creation processes, an understanding that their choices impact the purposes for which the information product will be used and the message it conveys | Learners who are developing their information-literate abilities:<br>• Understand that different methods of information dissemination with different purposes are available for their use |
| **Concept: information has value** | |
| Learners who are developing their information-literate abilities:<br>• Give credit to the original ideas of others through proper attribution and citation<br>• Understand that intellectual property is a legal and social construct that varies by culture<br>• Articulate the purpose and distinguishing characteristics of copyright, fair use, open access, and the public domain<br>• Make informed choices regarding their online actions in full awareness of issues related to privacy and the commodification of personal information | Learners who are developing their information-literate abilities:<br>• Respect the original ideas of others<br>• Value the skills, time, and effort needed to produce knowledge<br>• See themselves as contributors to the information marketplace rather than only consumers of it<br>• Are inclined to examine their own information privilege |

*(Continued)*

**Table 2.3** (Continued)

| Knowledge practices | Dispositions |
|---|---|
| *Concept: research as inquiry* | |
| Learners who are developing their information-literate abilities:<br>• Use various research methods, based on need, circumstance, and type of inquiry<br>• Monitor gathered information and assess for gaps or weaknesses | Learners who are developing their information-literate abilities:<br>• Follow ethical and legal guidelines in gathering and using information<br>• Demonstrate intellectual humility (ie, recognize their own intellectual or experiential limitations) |
| *Concept: scholarship as conversation* | |
| Learners who are developing their information-literate abilities:<br>• Cite the contributing work of others in their own information production | Learners who are developing their information-literate abilities:<br>• Understand the responsibility that comes with entering the conversation through participatory channels |
| *Concept: searching as strategic exploration* | |
| Learners who are developing their information-literate abilities:<br>• Identify interested parties, such as scholars, organizations, governments, and industries, who might produce information about a topic and then determine how to access that information | Learners who are developing their information-literate abilities:<br>• Realize that information sources vary greatly in content and format and have varying relevance and value, depending on the needs and nature of the search |

## 2.5 ETHICAL PRINCIPLES FOR INFORMATION LITERACY

According to Severson (1997), ethical behavior is a "discipline of thinking" (p. 9) that enables us to select the appropriate action in situations that range from simple to complex. While it may be simple to identify right and wrong behavior in situations where we have experience through our upbringing, it can be more challenging in new or complex situations. The expanding world of technology continues to present seemingly new and complex opportunities that outrun our experience.

Applying a discipline of ethical thinking to all situations invokes a more structured and deliberative kind of critical thinking (Severson, 1997, p. 8).

And, critical thinking includes ethical reflection that allows us to place events and situations in a principled context. Ethical behavior does not replace morality or the law, but "it can help guide and educate our moral instincts; steer us away from uncompromising positions; and improve our moral vocabulary so that we might talk and listen better" (p. 13).

A principled approach to ethical behavior provides flexible guidelines for our actions that furnish insights to be applied in specific situations. They enable a deliberative process of application so that informed, creative, and sometimes individualized actions can be taken to fit a particular circumstance. Teaching students ethical principles provides an internal as opposed to external control over their actions, along with a practical understanding of the law where it is appropriate. Severson (1997) identifies four principles of information ethics which can be used to direct responsible behavior in the use of information:

1. Respect for intellectual property;
2. Respect for privacy;
3. Fair representation;
4. Nonmaleficence (doing no harm).

Each of these principles will be examined with emphasis on engaging students toward understanding how they apply to individuals and situations.

### 2.5.1 Principle of Respect for Intellectual Property

The arena of intellectual property includes a consideration of information as property. At the simplistic end of the spectrum the perspective of information as a commodity relates to being able to identify who "owns" the information or information product. This becomes more complex as "ownership" becomes harder to establish with digital products or when information is reworked into new information products. A determination of intellectual property includes validating or determining the authenticity and reliability of information and presents opportunities to consider the purpose of creating information products and the associated value. According to Warlick (2009) "the ultimate value [of information] is based on its accuracy, validity, and reliability—on its authority" (p. 145).

Rapidly expanding technological developments may make it challenging to determine the authority of information. Where print publications provide hardcopy editions with static publication data, the digital environment makes information more accessible and more susceptible to manipulation. In the digital environment users can easily operate individually or within groups as information creators, producers, or consumers. Information can be plagiarized more easily and disseminated instantly.

Warlick (2009) suggests that "the best way to help students understand and appreciate information as valuable property is to make them property owners" (p. 140). This could involve having students place the copyright text (Copyright © date by *student name*) at the bottom of the pages, artwork, or media they produce. Discussing the effort it took to produce the product and the courtesy associated with giving credit or asking permission to use the intellectual and creative ideas of others is a way of personalizing the value of information. Students should be encouraged to learn from others, challenge the ideas of others, and explore extensively while acknowledging the work of others in the appropriate way: citations, acknowledgments, footnotes, references, bibliographies.

Conversations with students and class assignments can identify and include specific intellectual property laws such as copyright, fair use, trademarks, and patents along with the value of providing open access to information and the options available under Creative Commons licensing. Consequences associated with unacceptable behaviors such as fraud, theft, deceit, plagiarism, and withholding the results of research can be discussed under the principle of respect for intellectual property.

### 2.5.2 Principle of Respect for Privacy

Related to the principle of respect for intellectual property is the principle of respect for privacy. As Bodi (1998) notes "the individual decides who has the right or freedom to share in his or her activities or deliberations" (p. 461). Controlling those rights is challenging in a digital environment, and students must learn how to protect their personal information and respect the privacy of others.

Libraries defend the right to privacy through protection of student's circulation records, and a discussion of how personal data profiles are stored in databases for use by other agencies is an important aspect of the respect for privacy. Respect infers personal responsibility and that responsibility extends to being aware and cautious about what we share, how we share, and where that information is located. Privacy policies are distributed regularly by credit card companies, banking institutions, and online vendors. The consequences of inappropriate sharing of what should be considered private information can be seen with examples of organizations firing employees for inappropriate online displays of personal information, educators being chastised for posting unprofessional photos of themselves in online public spaces, and identity theft of personal data from supposedly encrypted databases. Efforts to protect information integrity, confidentiality, and availability can often conflict with the desire for the benefits of information sharing. Respect for privacy is also a respect for self.

### 2.5.3 Principle of Fair Representation

Trusting that the product you purchase will function as advertised is an example of the principle of fair representation. We should be able to rely on the information that is presented and trust that if products, such as downloadable software, do not behave as advertised, the vendor will accept responsibility and be accountable. Liability standards should ensure that product risks are mitigated and warranties should provide a form of insurance against product failures. This implies that vendors are honest in their efforts to deliver quality products and accept the consequences for any mistakes. Discussions of client–vendor relationships and, by extension, student–student relationships, place the responsibility for honest transactions in the personal realm.

Presenting opportunities for students to understand the implication of manipulating information, even under the guise of creative misrepresentation, ensures that the principle of fair representation is understood and endorsed.

### 2.5.4 Principle of Nonmaleficence (Doing no Harm)

Adopting the principle of nonmaleficence means, at a minimum, that "we must never do anything that might contribute to the decline of another person's life or affairs" (Severson, 1997, p. 108). This implies taking responsibility for our actions and understanding the impact of our information interactions, regardless of the environment in which they occur. For example, some people may find it easy to rant and rave via email but wouldn't consider such behavior in person.

Cyberbullying becomes a convenient method of intimidation because of the distance between persons and the presumed anonymity of the instigator. The impact of violating another person's privacy and causing harm must be placed in the personal arena where students have an opportunity to reflect on the purpose and consequences of malevolent acts.

The principle of doing no harm extends to an understanding of the impact on society. The unethical abuse of information, through computer viruses, hacking, malware, and phishing, is pervasive and expensive. The impact of these actions can be discussed in the context of adopting the principle of nonmaleficence, and appropriate actions should manifest themselves in the realm of digital citizenship. As Warlick (2009) states:

> Information is power, and 21st century literacy equips children and adults, learners and teachers with powerful tools. We have at our disposal a global electronic library of information, much of it coming out of our own communities. We are increasingly gaining access to potent digital tools that can access, alter, and communicate that information in infinite and persuasive ways. (p. 148)

Abusing the ideas of others, tampering with or distorting the ideas of others, or using information to cause harm violates an individual's place in the community of learners and can be harmful to society as a whole. Our place in the larger context of society and our civic responsibilities begin with an acceptance and understanding of self and self-respect. Providing assignments, activities, and discussions that enable perception, processing, and comprehension takes time. But the benefit of becoming reflective thinkers who can tackle issues and synthesize information is paramount. Ethical decisions require rational decision making.

## 2.6 LEARNING ENVIRONMENT

To openly discuss, confront, and address the ethical challenges in the global world of information, it is important to create a learning environment that models and honors ethical principles while guiding inquiry and encouraging creativity. Much of this depends on the skills, behaviors and attitudes of educators and the culture of the learning environment. Importance should be placed on establishing a learning environment that:
- Encourages the exchange of ideas and concepts;
- Offers a safe place for the debate of ideas;
- Instructs students on the principles underlying the ethical use of information;
- Equips students with the skills and abilities to be information literate;
- Reinforces the need for reflection and synthesis;
- Respects the privacy of individuals;
- Encourages creativity, ingenuity, and lifelong learning.

The learning environment for a community of learners can be established in face-to-face contact or online. Certainly there is a difference in those environments in terms of physical proximity, but a learning environment that nurtures lifelong learning can develop a sense of community that enables open discussion and teaches the ethical use of information.

The difference in environments and potential difference in the sense of "community" is an important discussion point: our social software "spaces" can create communities of practice that enable productive exchanges of information and inspire creativity. Points of netiquette within these spaces are worth debating and, in some communities of practice, a code of behavior will be established to ensure that everyone is treated respectfully. In that way, the likelihood of a dual world where behavior in one does not necessarily reflect behavior in another is diminished. The speed of communication can also alter the relationship among community members. People may not take the time to reflect on the possibility or implications of the unethical use of information. Sensitivity to personal behavior in these various circumstances can be taught.

## 2.7 TEACHING ETHICS AS A MIL SKILL

Teaching ethical information literacy skills involves considering how to construct our instruction to meet our understanding of how students learn. Two practical models that enable a deep personalization of ethics as an information literacy skill are: informed learning (Bruce, 2008) and guided inquiry (Kuhlthau et al., 2012), based on the information search process (Kuhlthau, 1985, 2004).

Informed learning "proposes that teaching and learning must (a) bring about new ways of experiencing and using information, and (b) engage students with the information practices that are relevant to their discipline or profession" (Bruce, 2008, p. ix). The broad theoretical framework for informed learning consists of six frames that present lenses to focus on how students experience learning in various contexts (see Table 2.4). This emphasis on experience resonates with the constructivist theory of learning that posits we construct meaning and knowledge through interaction between experiences and ideas. Providing learning experiences and providing opportunities to reflect on those experiences deepens student understanding and enables a stronger, more personal conceptual knowledge of the world.

**Table 2.4** Six frames for informed learning of the ethical use of information (Bruce, 2008)

| | |
|---|---|
| Content | What should learners know about the subject?<br>Objective: Students will understand ethics related to the use of information and know the resources available for learning and applying the ethical use of information<br>Activities: Lessons dealing with key content in ethics, including relevant information sources and search techniques |
| Competency | What should learners be able to do?<br>Objective: Students will be able to make ethical decisions in the context of their information world<br>Activities: Build ethical competence by working with a series of ethics cases, determining the key aspects of each case and making decisions about what action would be appropriate |
| Learning to learn | What does it mean to think like an informed learner?<br>Objective: Use a range of resources to engage with ethical cases and reflect on how your use of information has influenced engagement with the cases<br>Activities: Students work with a series of ethical cases and conduct their own research. Encourage them to work with a range of types of information, people, blogs, research articles, and their own experiences. Ask them to think regularly about what they are learning and how they are using information to learn |
| Personal relevance | What good is ethical information literacy to me?<br>Objective: Students reflect on how ethics and the information processes they are using may influence their personal lives<br>Activities: Students work with a series of ethical cases and conduct their own research. Encourage them to work with a range of types of information, people, blogs, research articles, and their own experiences. Ask them to think regularly about what they are learning, how they are using information to learn, and where ethical decisions are being made |
| Social impact | How does the ethical use of information impact society?<br>Objective: Students consider how different ethical decisions may impact society<br>Activities: Students work with a series of ethical cases and conduct their own research. Students are asked to consider how their information-use processes are helping them to see the social implications embedded in the cases |
| Relational | Focus on bringing about awareness of the critical ways of seeing or experiencing<br>Objective: Students consider the decisions they make in a specific case from a range of perspectives, identifying differences between their own and other's views<br>Activities: Students articulate their own views about the cases and see the different views emerging among peers. Students identify significant differences in the ways in which matters are dealt with and identify what they consider to be relevant information and how that information informs their views |

The use of scenarios or cases is fundamental to engaging students with their learning processes and providing students with the opportunity to interact with others, and other perspectives, while reflecting on their responses to a variety of situations. The presentation of scenarios can be used as specific lessons directed toward an understanding of the ethical use of information. Or, they can be used within a research and inquiry framework to operationalize ethical information literacy initiatives at the point of need.

The guided inquiry design framework (Kuhlthau et al., 2012) invites educators to construct the inquiry process as a model, based on Kuhlthau's (1985, 2004) information search process (ISP), with educators participating in the process by guiding and encouraging inquiry. The ISP model is shaped by three realms of behaviors: *affective* (feelings), *cognitive* (thoughts), and *physical* (actions and strategies). The guided inquiry design framework (see Table 2.5) constitutes a series of eight phases that address these behaviors by involving the researcher in a process guided by educators that provides specific opportunities for personal reflection. Reflection is directed toward personal goals, reactions to the experience, skills learned, and processes used. Thus, research is experienced beyond the sheer rigid technicalities of finding information, and involves the searcher (feelings, thoughts, and actions and strategies) through guided steps to understanding what they have accomplished. Using this model effectively integrates the *Six Frames for Informed Learning* in a practical and flexible model of learning.

With the guided inquiry framework as our reference, the entire inquiry experience, unfolding over several sessions, could focus entirely on understanding ethics and build knowledge of ethical principles. Or, specific phases could offer opportunities to present learning through various lenses (informed learning frame):

- *Content* that builds knowledge of ethical principles could be woven into the immerse phase;
- *Competency* can be built with search and evaluation strategies to locate reliable information about a topic and included in the explore, identify, and gather phases;
- *Learning to learn* can be emphasized in the gather and evaluate phases through use of the inquiry logs, inquiry journals, reflection, and self-assessment;
- *Personal relevance* can be the focus of the enquiry phase;

Table 2.5 Guided inquiry design summary (Kuhlthau et al., 2012)

| Phase | Activity | Librarian role | Teacher role |
|---|---|---|---|
| 1. Open | Set an invitational tone with a short but powerful learning event to spark student interest and elicit prior knowledge. Examples: dramatic video, object, photograph, art image. Full group activity | Lead and participate. Carefully consider what will engage this particular group of students at this point in time | Each inquiry community and each inquiry is different so contribute knowledge of this inquiry community to build the opener. Lead and participate |
| 2. Immerse | Guide students to connect with the content and to discover interesting ideas to explore further. Don't overwhelm students with too many facts. Examples: Consider stimulating experiences, such as an episode of https://learninglab.org/ or a television show, reading a stimulating text or a scenario. Combine full group activity with smaller group inquiry circles so students can discuss further. Individually, students begin an inquiry journal | Facilitate the organization and delivery of the experiences. Model the inquiry stance by accepting different perspectives, incomplete ideas, and speculations. Listen for personal connections and interesting ideas. Encourage all voices and provide a supportive and safe environment | Facilitate the organization and delivery of the experiences. Model the inquiry stance by accepting different perspectives, incomplete ideas, and speculations. Listen for personal connections and interesting ideas. Encourage all voices and provide a supportive and safe environment |
| 3. Explore | Students browse various sources of information to explore interesting ideas and prepare to develop their inquiry questions. Explore ideas rather than accumulate facts. Relax, read, and reflect. Utilize inquiry logs and the inquiry journal. Individual time and group inquiry circles | Guide students to browse and scan a variety of sources, read when they find something interesting, and reflect on questions that begin to shape their inquiry | Contribute to a calm, reflective tone, not rushed or deadline-oriented. Help to create an environment that values a thoughtful, attentive, interested approach |

| | | | |
|---|---|---|---|
| 4. Identify | Construct an inquiry question that will frame the rest of the inquiry: What is interesting to me? What are my learning goals? How much information is available? How much time do I have? Utilize inquiry logs and the inquiry journal. Individual time and group inquiry circles | Introduce strategies to enable each student to sort through information and ideas to clearly articulate a meaningful inquiry question | Look for evidence that the inquiry is going to move into deep learning |
| 5. Gather | Students collect detailed information from a variety of sources; a time of comprehensive searching that encompasses locating, evaluating, and using a variety of sources of information. Utilize inquiry logs and the inquiry journal. Individual time and group inquiry circles to reflect on their process | Guide students in locating, evaluating, and using information. Concepts approach to ethics and information literacy that introduces skills and strategies | Guide learners to choose what is personally meaningful and compelling about their inquiry question in the information sources |
| 6. Create | Organize learning into a creative presentation. Synthesize all the ideas and reflect on what they have learned. Inquiry chart, inquiry logs, inquiry journal. Individual time and group time. Product examples: videos, blogs, web pages, Power Points, speeches, shadow puppet play, scrapbook, exhibition, interactive activity, artwork | Guide students in creating a meaningful, interesting, clearly articulated, well-documented presentation that tells the story of what they have learned and provides appropriate attribution | Guide students toward synthesizing and communicating their learning |

*(Continued)*

Table 2.5 (Continued)

| Phase | Activity | Librarian role | Teacher role |
|---|---|---|---|
| 7. Share | Share the product that was created, to show what they learned. Individual contributions, inquiry circles, and full group time | Organize share sessions to provide the best conditions for students to learn substantial content from each other | Encourage students to formally present their ideas and help them voice their new knowledge |
| 8. Evaluate | Evaluate achievement of learning goals. Reflection and self-assessment. Analyze data sources. Conference sessions with individual students and full group to explore student learning about process and content | Guide students toward an awareness of how they learned through the process | Involve students in the task of evaluating their learning process |
| Leaders evaluate and reflect | Librarian and teacher discuss what went well, what could be done differently, and plan for next time | | |

- *Social impact* could be included in the create and share phases as a way to encourage the identification of ethical principles and discussion with peers;
- *Relational* awareness of various perspectives regarding ethical situations can be built in the open, share, and evaluate phases.

Being mindful of the six frames for informed learning and the guided inquiry process provides a solid framework for building the ethical foundation while building information literacy skills.

## 2.8 INTEGRATING ETHICS IN TEACHING INFORMATION LITERACY

An information literacy program in a school setting typically focuses on developing the skills for evaluating websites and providing correct attribution for sources. Now, educators can take a broader view and look for those opportunities to anchor the skills within a broader context:

- Move from information literacy instruction as library skills to embedding the process of learning to learn within all elements of interaction with students;
- Place ethical skills instruction in the context of the broader process of information literacy;
- Include ethical scenarios (Denison, 2015) for discussion and personal relevance (http://www.goodcharacter.com/dilemma/archive.html);
- Identify resources for ethical information practices:
  - Common sense education: digital citizenship (https://www.commonsensemedia.org/educators/curriculum);
  - Edutopia's Bullying Prevention (http://www.edutopia.org/blogs/tag/bullying-prevention);
  - Ribble's (2015) Digital Citizenship (http://www.digitalcitizenship.net/);
- Focus on learning outcomes (goal-oriented);
- Motivate for life-long learning.

Other techniques and processes can be used to operationalize ethical information literacy initiatives by weaving competencies into the fabric of the educational curriculum:

- Program approach:
  - Lessons;
  - Series of lessons.
- Vertical alignment K-12: design learning experiences that build knowledge from one grade to the next.

- Integrated reinforcement by integrating learning across the curriculum and across grade levels; iterative approach.
- Reflective learning by encouraging group discussion and personal reflection.
- An inquiry approach that encourages questioning, seeking, and curiosity.
- An inquiry stance that is modeled by displaying the construction of inquiries, exhibiting curiosity, and demonstrating search strategies.
- Presenting useful questions that evoke ethics as an information literacy skill.

An ethical approach to the use of information can be taught within the context of a specific information need, whether it is a research project for a college level or high school assignment, or a simple inquiry of interest from a student in a primary grade. While methods of instruction vary, to be truly effective they depend on three elements: integration (within and across the curriculum), reflection (personally and interactively), and reinforcement (repeated exposure to ethical principles).

As each inquiry opportunity develops and unfolds, educators can encourage an orientation toward ethical principles. As we guide students to understand the ethical foundation underpinning information literacy, the following questions are useful for consideration:

- Is it illegal? (then it probably is unethical);
- Does it violate ethical principles (which ones)?
- Does it bother your conscience or violate your personal values and principles or those of others around you?
- Does it look as though someone is likely to be harmed? (the someone could be you);
- If something terrible happens, could you defend your actions?
- Would this practice continue if it were publicized, for example in the local or college newspaper?

By repeatedly opening the discussion of ethical principles, engaging students through various scenarios, providing the skills to effectively search, evaluate, and determine reliability, encouraging personal reflection, and illuminating the consequences personally and as a society, we can build competency for the ethical use of information.

If we are able to build competency within the K-12 environment, the stage should be set for responsible action beyond high school. Equipped with the necessary skills and an ethical orientation to the use of information the next phases of student growth can include increasingly complex situations where students feel competent in their ability to understand and respond responsibly. Realistically, this foundation is not always firmly established and the next phase of student learning, at college or university, requires that students understand the research process and appreciate the requirements for and consequences of ethical decision making.

At the college level, faculty rely on academic librarians to provide an orientation to conducting research, obtaining materials, and documenting sources appropriately. Academic integrity policies explicitly define the expectations and consequences for not following these policies. As Sciammarella (2009) observes: "The librarian can function as an intermediary in terms of introducing the student to scholarly information and the practice of acceptable documentation" (p. 24). The librarian can also function as a collaborator with the teaching faculty to develop proactive strategies to address ethical issues that correlate to the educational goals of each academic subject and the respective assignments.

## 2.9 CONCLUSION

Where does this leave educators throughout the K-20 learning environment? First, it implies that we must be knowledgeable:
- Understand the developmental stages of young people, along with their evolving ability to deal with increasingly more complex ethical issues;
- Accept that providing the socially correct answer to a dilemma does not imply understanding of the underlying ethical issues;
- Be prepared to assist students move from an egocentric perspective to an understanding of different perspectives by investing the time in preparing and sharing decision-making situations that engage students and provide the opportunity to select an appropriate course of action;
- Apply a variety of teaching methods that respond to the variety of student needs and comfort levels: for example, brainstorming, debates, discussions, role-playing, simulations;
- Stay informed about legislative issues related to technology access;
- Stay knowledgeable about the burgeoning technology applications and their use and potential misuse.

Second, be proactive:
- Advocate for regulations and laws that encourage student learning;
- Engage other educators in conversations about teaching strategies, potential areas of ethical concern, and educational resources;

- Educate yourself on the appropriate use of social media and ways to demonstrate a responsible digital footprint;
- Maintain professional development through professional organizations, conferences, print and online publications, and educators blogs, and Twitter posts;
- Seek collaborators within your educational community to coordinate approaches to developing ethical information literacy practices.

Ultimately, as we guide students to develop information competences and become lifelong learners, we are reinforcing skills and attitudes that encourage responsible action; placing ethical principles within the context of information literacy skills may be an effective way of guiding student behavior toward ethical information literacy practices. This becomes an ongoing journey, for ourselves and for our students.

## REFERENCES

American Association of School Librarians [AASL]. (2007). *Standards for the 21st-century learner*. Chicago, IL: ALA.

American Library Association [ALA]. (1989). *Presidential committee on information literacy final report*. Chicago, IL: ALA. Retrieved from: http://www.ala.org/acrl/publications/whitepapers/presidential.

Association of College and Research Libraries [ACRL]. (2000). *Information literacy competency standards*. Chicago, IL: ACRL. Retrieved from: https://arizona.openrepository.com/arizona/bitstream/10150/105645/1/standards.pdf.

Association of College and Research Libraries [ACRL]. (2015). *Framework for information literacy for higher education*. Chicago, IL: ACRL. Retrieved from: http://www.ala.org/acrl/sites/ala.org.acrl/files/content/issues/infolit/Framework_ILHE.pdf.

Bodi, S. (1998). Ethics and information technology: Some principles to guide students. *The Journal of Academic Librarianship, 24*(6), 459–463.

Bruce, C. S. (2008). *Informed learning*. Chicago, IL: ACRL.

Canadian Library Association [CLA]. (2014). *Standards of practice for school library learning commons in Canada*. Ottawa, ON: CLA. Retrieved from: http://apsds.org/wp-content/uploads/Standards-of-Practice-for-SchoolLibrary-Learning-Commons-in-Canada-2014.pdf.

Denison, C. (2015). goodcharacter.com. Ethical dilemmas for classroom discussion: The daily dilemma archive. Retrieved from: http://www.goodcharacter.com/dilemma/archive.html.

European Council. (2006). Key competences for lifelong learning. EUR-Lex Access to European Union Law. Retrieved from http://eur-lex.europa.eu/legal-content/EN/TXT/?uri=URISERV:c11090.

International Federation of Library Associations (IFLA). (2006). *Guidelines on information literacy for lifelong learning*. The Hague: IFLA. Retrieved from: http://www.ifla.org/files/assets/information-literacy/publications/ifla-guidelines-en.pdf.

Kuhlthau, C. C. (1985). *Teaching the library research process* (2nd ed.). Metuchen, NJ: Scarecrow Press.

Kuhlthau, C. C. (2004). *Seeking meaning: A process approach to library and information services* (2nd ed.). Westport, CT: Libraries Unlimited.

Kuhlthau, C. C., Maniotes, L. K., & Caspari, A. K. (2012). *Guided inquiry design: A framework for inquiry in your school*. Santa Barbara, CA: Libraries Unlimited.
Ribble, M. (2015). Digital citizenship: Using technology appropriately. Retrieved from: http://www.digitalcitizenship.net/.
Sciammarella, S. (2009). Making a difference: Library and teaching faculty working together to develop strategies in dealing with student plagiarism. *Community & Junior College Libraries, 15*, 23–34.
Severson, R. J. (1997). *The principles of information ethics*. Armonk, NJ: M. E. Sharpe.
Warlick, D. F. (2009). *Redefining literacy 2.0*. Columbus, OH: Linworth Books.

# CHAPTER 3

# Promoting Civic Literacy in Teacher Education: A Framework for Personal and Professional Development

K. Flornes
Bergen University College, Bergen, Norway

*Cognition is beautiful, it is beautiful to know*

*John M. Hull (2015)*

## 3.1 INTRODUCTION

Civic literacy plays a key role in the development and maintenance of democratic societies. Teachers need to have the skills and understanding required to help children, from an early age, to be motivated to take an active part in democratic activities in schools and in the wider society.

Media and information competences are key instruments for the construction of civic literacy.

The UNESCO (2012) Media and Information Literacy Curriculum for Teachers is a flexible framework for supporting civic literacy programs at every level from kindergarten to higher education.

Modern technology gives individuals the possibility of participating in educational activities and of receiving, using, and sharing information of various kinds with few obstacles or limitations. This situation has widely influenced not only the teaching and learning activities in our educational organizations, but how, where, and when learning takes place. From an early age, children are using new technologies to learn, understand and participate in the world. The learning takes place in formal, noninformal, and informal ways in various contexts, a fact that has influenced many teacher education institutions in Norway and beyond and that has changed the way that we educate teachers. Initial teacher education no longer has a specific ending point; it is the start of a lifelong professional and personal learning process. Because of our rapidly changing societies, teachers have to work continuously to improve their knowledge, skills, and competences. New technologies entail new learning strategies and offer multiple challenges in schools and classrooms which are becoming more and more diverse and multicultural.

There is also the important and pertinent question of ethics. As information comes from so many sources, both filtered and unfiltered, there is a need even in kindergarten and primary schools to develop ethical guidelines and theories for a digital ethical understanding and reflection.

Sandos (2014) did a case study in some Norwegian kindergartens for his doctoral dissertation. His aim was to discover how preschool children are educated in order to become robust and empathic users of internet resources. He found a significant knowledge gap in this area. Children as information and communications technology (ICT) users seem to be a neglected group in research projects and in the debate about ICT ethics. Consequently, the formation of the knowledge construction processes in teachers, both in college and in practice as teachers in kindergartens and schools, has to be focused on issues connected to the ethical and responsible use of the internet and the social media; these must be critically investigated, discussed, and learnt. Sandos recommends a digital training program including digital ethics for preschool teachers and proposes that this training should be a compulsory part of teacher education.

In order to assess the quality of information and judge its relevance, teachers need critical thinking and reflection (Brookfield, 1995). They also have to ask themselves how they can use information in ethically acceptable ways and how to help their pupils to do the same. As professional teachers they need to cooperate with their pupils to create appropriate approaches to deal with ethical questions related to a responsible and ethical use of ICT.

## 3.2 MEDIA AND INFORMATION LITERACY AND HUMAN RIGHTS

In recent publications from the Council of Europe (2014a, 2014b), media literacy is described as *the critical, responsible, and beneficial use of the media environment* and as one of the key competences for the construction of sustainable democratic societies. A sustainable democratic society needs citizens with a set of basic skills, called transversal skills, which are composed of the attitudes, skills, and knowledge central to the education and actions of concerned and responsible citizens. For teachers, transversal skills will be foremost among their specific competences in academic subjects, particular skills that they will be encouraged to develop within themselves. The Pestalozzi program of The Council of Europe offers a number of publications with the aim of supporting teachers' development of transversal skills (see, for example, Council of Europe, 2008, 2011, 2012; Huber & Mompoint-Gaillard, 2011). The Council's most recent publication titled *Tasks for Democracy* (Council of Europe, 2016b) offers 60 different activities to learn and assess transversal attitudes, skills, and knowledge.

In a democratic society all citizens ought to have free access to all sorts of information on-line and off-line. The right to information and freedom of expression has to be viewed and implemented as a human right for all, regardless of age, race, gender, religions, worldviews, positions, or nationality. Nevertheless, freedom of expression has its limits, which should be known and respected by all citizens. In 2014, the Council of Europe initiated the *No Hate Speech online Campaign*, a campaign that will last until the end of 2017. Hate speech uses social media to promote racism and discrimination (Council of Europe, 2014a). Extreme and radical movements use the internet to spread hate and propaganda and manipulate young people to take part in conflicts and wars causing fear, uncertainty, and destruction all over the world. We live in a digital culture that affects us in many different ways, economic, political, social, and cultural. For example, in Norway if elderly people have not become familiar with this new digital culture, they have problems paying their bills and fulfilling other social obligations.

Teachers as facilitators of knowledge and skills have to learn how they can construct more inclusive relationships with the learners in order to interact in positive and empathic ways with them (Brudal, 2014). Lisbeth Brudal is a Norwegian psychologist and expert in positive psychology. She recommends *empathic communication* as an appropriate and effective dialogical tool in teacher–learner interactions. As violent radicalization is spreading all over the world, teachers have to build more inclusive and sustainable interactions and relationships with their learners as a way of fighting it. Properly educated teachers will be able, with help, to address this problem and find a solution for this challenge. It has to be faced by a whole-school action plan approach in which school leaders, teachers, learners, and parents cooperate to develop a safe and inclusive learning environment for all learners. This challenge is too difficult for individual teachers to solve on their own.

Children and young people are already competent and enthusiastic *users* of social media, but they have to be educated to become *responsible* ICT users who turn away from the use of hate speech on the internet. The key disseminators of this education are teachers who are media- and information-literate and able to interact with learners in democratic ways.

This education has to start from the prospective teacher's first day in teacher education, developed and expanded in the college lessons, in teaching and learning activities, in practice schools, and in the construction of personal knowledge bases, skills, and competences. Few teacher education institutions so far have been able to promote this education systematically or to include all educators, students, and staff in this process (Flornes, 2007).

According to the documents from the Pestalozzi Program in the Council of Europe (2011, 2014b), in the past two decades media users have changed from recipients and consumers of messages, to active producers of content of a much wider range than previously imagined. This shift is widely felt in teacher education, for students have become more selective and reflective users of internet resources and more creative in composing their own presentations both in group works and plenary sessions. They are more professional in the production of the presentations, which have become less based on resources from the internet and more drawn from their own authentic work, for example, creative compositions of multimodal texts, pictures, drawings, and video-clips. This is evidence that MIL competences can afford and fuel autonomy in student teachers' professional development and stimulate their capacity to be creative and innovative.

## 3.3 TEACHER EDUCATION IN NORWAY

In 2010, a new program for teacher education was introduced in Norway. This program is a 4-year course of studies, involving a bachelor's degree with a thesis after 3 years, and a fourth year leading to a diploma in teaching. There is also the possibility of a master's degree after a fifth year of study. From 2017 this option will be compulsory, requiring all teachers who are educated and trained to work in the primary and lower secondary schools in Norway to obtain a master's degree for their professional work as teachers.

The 2010 program offers two models, one called GLU 1-7 for student teachers who want to work with children in the first 7 years of primary school. The other called GLU 5-10 is for students who want to be qualified to teach both in primary school 5—7 grades and in lower secondary schools 8—10 grades. The compulsory subjects in teacher education in Norway are Norwegian and mathematics, 30 credits each, and pedagogies, a 60-credit subject composed of four 15-credit units, one for each of the 4-year-long program.

In the first 2 years of this program, students have to choose to study a particular school subject according to their individual interests. These subjects are:
- English;
- Physical education;
- Domestic science;
- Music;
- Natural science;
- Religious education (RE);
- Social science.

As the writing of assignments is a focus of the 2010 teacher education program, which entails a bachelor's degree based on a thesis, teacher educators have become more concerned about information literacy and ways to educate information-literate teachers (Bårnes & Løkse, 2014).

My MIL investigation took place in the first 2-year course of GLU 1-7 from 2010 to 2012 with students who had chosen to study RE. It started as a pilot project but gradually it was implemented as a model for the RE program in the subsequent years of 2012—16. RE is a 30-credit subject, 15 credits for each year of the 2-year-long program.

## 3.4 EDUCATING THE INFORMATION-LITERATE TEACHER: A PILOT PROJECT

In the department of RE that I belong to, a colleague educator and I decided to improve our practice. We were responsible for the 2-year RE program for student teachers in GLU 1-7, student teachers who would qualify for the teaching of grades 1—7 in primary school. Consequently, from the induction phase of the new model, we started to work more closely, not only within our own subject but bringing in an ICT colleague and librarians from the college library. From the start of our project, experts, librarians, and practitioners were part of our cooperative team.

The county library, the director, and a chief librarian were contacted and agreed to contribute to the project offering both expert help and financial support. This paved the way for us to ask trainers in schools to join us since we could then cover the cost of the time that they spent on the project.

After these initial preparations, we were able to develop a project called *"Educating the information-literate teacher"*. As teacher educators, we had considerable experience of teaching freshmen in teacher education, many years of cooperation in RE courses, and a shared conviction that the process of academic writing, especially in higher education, is a very efficient learning strategy and an excellent way to learn. From the beginning of the project this certainty was confirmed. Academic writing is a good way to learn, an argument, widely reported in the research literature (Imhof & Picard, 2009). Sigrid Grøtterud in her doctoral studies found that students in teacher education improved their personal and professional development by writing. She formed groups of students who cooperated in the writing process by using what she calls "love and critique" as the guiding perspectives of reference and evaluation (Grøtterud, 2011). By using both a positive and a critical regard in the proofreading and editing of each other's texts, students were able to improve their written work considerably. The reading of their written texts and discussion of their quality and what measures to take to improve them were good exercises for developing a professional language and using the specific concepts related to particular themes. They then learned to discuss various issues related to the teaching and learning of these themes. This approach also challenged them to cooperate in a range of situations in which they had to negotiate and reach a conclusion based on the best possible arguments.

Piloting the *"Educating the information-literate teacher"* project convinced us that the process of writing assignments had a great influence on teacher students' professional development. In their feedback during the course and in the last metatexts in the exam portfolio we read a number of texts from students who shared their experiences, such as the following:

> It was when I started to write my assignments after attending the academic writing and source searching course in the library that I was empowered and inspired to develop my own knowledge base. Gradually in this writing process my self-perception changed and I began to see myself as a future competent leader of children's learning, development, and education.
> 
> **Quote from a student.**
>
> For me the best learning outcome in RE has come from the writing of assignments. In addition to the improvements in academic writing, it is an excellent

*way of achieving knowledge and constructing a personal knowledge base. The academic library on BUC's new campus is an excellent place to learn. The RE shelves are filled with books to be explored to find the relevant literature that can be used for my work. The library course was excellent and gave me a useful insight into the extended digital resources to be used for my assignment writing. Thus I developed a solid platform for the writing of the compulsory assignments linked to the topics presented in the lectures and in the various learning activities, all with a theoretical part and a didactic one.*

**Quote from a student.**

Encouraged by such positive feedback from the students and by our own experiences and evaluations, we decided to develop a project about the information-literate teacher and investigate how the competences of information literacy could be promoted in initial teacher education through RE. We wanted to develop a new model for the 2-year-long RE course based on cooperation, creative interactions, and democratic participation on all levels of the study. The main aim was to create a good learning community for student teachers and to include in this community librarians both from the college and from the schools where students had their practice. Therefore, we started to look for schools with good school libraries and staff members who wanted to improve both their libraries and their information literacy competences. We visited some practice schools and talked to the principals and the school librarians. All of them showed a positive interest in the project and agreed to participate.

In all these schools teachers wanted to improve the quality of their school libraries and improve the MIL competences among the teachers. Thus we could discuss and share a vision that student teachers in their school practice would be able to use to improve their information literacy in step with their learners by using the information literacy skills acquired in the college. In this way a continuous process of information literacy learning could take place in the practice schools by means of teaching and learning activities with pupils in the classroom.

The aim was to build a more constructive and sustainable bridge between the MIL taught and learnt in the college and that taught and learnt in schools. The education of teachers has several aims to fulfill—learning, learning to learn, and learning to teach (Palmer, 1998; Riedling, 2002). Therefore it is necessary to "ride two horses" at the same time to show student teachers, the teachers of the future, a clear coherence between theory and practice. After a period of discussion and planning we developed an action plan with a key focus on MIL.

## 3.5 THE CONSTRUCTION OF AN MIL APPROACH IN TEACHER EDUCATION

The work started by revising the RE program, curriculum, and working scheme. The main change we made was to compose a structured scheme for a portfolio, consisting of a number of compulsory assignments that were linked to some of the main RE themes presented during the term. The process of constructing a personal MIL knowledge base and achieving the necessary competences of academic writing to compile a portfolio starts from the first year of the students' study. The main focus in the induction phase is on MIL. By the end of the 2-year 30 credit course, the specific aim for students is to compile an exam portfolio containing one meta-reflective text and two texts selected by the student. These texts are the ones considered the best of all texts that they have written as evaluated and approved by the course leaders. The portfolio approach offers a pedagogical tool to acquire the skills of academic writing by submitting the required assignments. It also promotes reflection and critical thinking which are very important competences for an RE teacher who must teach this school subject, as the curriculum demands, in a pluralistic, objective, and critical way.

The project started with the cooperation of a group of teacher educators who from a variety of competences could constructively participate in a MIL approach—two RE teacher educators, an ICT specialist, and several librarians. We wanted to explore how we could work to improve our information literacy using the college's *It's Learning* program as our basic online learning platform. This learning platform is a shared learning and information arena for teacher educators in the teacher education college and for the teacher-mentors in practice schools.

In addition we found a library resource, a set of tutorials called *Search & Write*, to be a good instrument for our work (Torras & Sætre, 2009). "*Search & Write* is for all students who want to learn more about information gathering and academic writing, independent of institution and subject area" (see http://sokogskriv.no/en/). Since the college librarians are responsible for this program, we started to work closer with them.

Two college librarians gave a library and information literacy course, which both student teachers and RE teacher educators took. The aim was to develop new and more efficient skills in information literacy by using the online learning platform, the internet and social media such as Web 2.0, blogs, and Facebook. In addition to the library course, the ICT specialist arranged a workshop where students could improve their ICT skills, and the students constructed a blog to exchange their experiences and ideas.

Ethical questions regarding religions and worldview are of great interest in RE. Winje (2009) developed a tool for distinguishing which websites are of a quality appropriate for academic texts in RE. He named this tool for "the four Ss" to stand for the four different perspectives to adopt in analyzing internet resources which in Norwegian all start with S. The only perspective useful for an academic text is the one called "serious and objective"; the three others have a hidden agenda trying to manipulate and influence users one way or another. The contrast between the different websites made it very easy to pick out the one that could be used in an academic text. This problem was presented and discussed by the librarian who introduced the problem to the students, and the discussion continued in the subsequent RE teaching and learning activities.

In this interdisciplinary work, the *Search & Write* program became a common source of information concerning all of the "how" questions that can possibly be asked in the writing process. In addition we wanted the librarians to inform our students of interesting sources for their writing and to encourage them to develop a closer relationship with the librarians in the academic library. The main aim for this approach was to inspire our students to spend more time in the library and thus have sufficient opportunity to explore all the available resources for their work and become active users of the *Search & Write* program.

Information gathering and academic writing are key elements of the *Search & Write* program, a program which is continuously revised and improved by a team of expert researchers from abroad who interview users, students, and staff for regular revisions of the program. The program is designed for libraries in higher institution organizations as a tool of MIL that is accurate, reliable, and updated for use in the academic community.

## 3.6 RELIGIOUS EDUCATION AND MIL

Early in the project, we found that RE, as a compulsory school subject, is excellent when it comes to the development of a MIL project. RE comprises a wide range of topics and offers an excellent framework for students to explore a variety of issues related to religions, worldviews, ethics, art, philosophy, human rights, citizenship, and democracy (Council of

Europe, 2014b). For students asked to write the compulsory assignments on an academic level, the competences of information literacy play an important role. The RE curriculum invites student teachers to start the process of developing these competences. The first step is to raise an awareness among future teachers that they must include in their vision of becoming a professional teacher a definition and a view of what is implied by being information literate and the way to become so. The *Search & Write* tutorial offers the following definition of an information-literate person:

> An information-literate person is someone who knows when and why they need information, how to find the information and how to evaluate, use, and communicate the information in an ethical way.

The need for information is closely related to the assignments process. As soon as the topic of the work is defined, the writer has to search for information to inform the writing. In the pilot project of MIL, the first assignment was given by the librarians who also took care of the evaluation of the assignment. In this way the knowledge of MIL had to be put into action immediately after the MIL course. This procedure created a relationship between the students and the librarians and motivated students to make more extended use of the academic library and to ask the staff questions face-to-face in addition to asking questions on the online learning platform *It's Learning*.

In 2014, Bergen University College moved to a new campus with new buildings and new facilities. Thanks to these new opportunities, students developed new strategies for their learning. They could now bring their laptops into the library, find a place to work either individually or in groups, and ask the librarians for help when needed. The collection of books on the shelves was considerably increased, and they were displayed in a more informative and structured way, making it easier for students to search for and find what they needed. The library was extended to embrace all the libraries from the colleges of engineering, health, and teacher education, and a number of new librarians were appointed to serve this multitude of studies and subjects. The new librarians, many of them quite young, could offer guiding support in the research and writing process. For RE, the appointment of a new librarian with a master's degree in religious studies considerably improved what the library could offer in terms of guidance in the work and tasks of the RE students.

In 2007, Sætre, the first director of the new extended university library, investigated the role of the library in the students' construction and acquisition of knowledge. She related the shift in the work and role of librarians to the Norwegian Quality Reform, introduced in 2000–01. Traditionally the role of the librarians was to act as facilitators and mediators of knowledge and information, but since the implementation of the reform (2003), which gave more weight to academic writing and student-oriented learning activities, librarians have been asked to play a more active role in the students' learning and studies. Given that assignments are compulsory in all study programs from the first year, the competences of the librarians in the "search and write" phase of assignments have become very important.

Sætre (2007) emphasizes that there is a close connection between students' personal and professional development and the quality of the library for study and research, with support for the students from well-qualified librarians. This argument is widely reported in the RE-students' assessments in the metatexts of the exam portfolio, as the example below illiustrates:

> Because of the emphasis on assignments linked to key issues of the curriculum, I have improved my academic writing skills. The process of writing has always been one of my favorite activities and throughout my school years and in these 2 first years in higher education, I have found that writing is a very efficient learning method. As a freshman in higher education I have experienced that the writing of assignments has given me the opportunity to deepen my knowledge in specific RE topics and consider the issues from different perspectives. The information literacy courses given by the librarians afforded me the skills needed to write my assignments. The quality of the academic library gave me an excellent place to work, a number of analogue and digital resources and librarians who are available for questions and help. In this writing process I have improved my formal writing skills and gained security when it comes to references and quoting of various analogue and digital resources.
> **Quote from a student.**

This student is able to share her experiences of learning in an informative way: her first two years of teacher education in the area of RE have helped her to become a good and reflective teacher. To be open to new ideas, and thus find opportunities to consider specific issues from different perspectives, is a very useful and important competence, not only for an RE teacher, but for all teachers. During this process, as this student reports, students reflect within themselves and construct fresh knowledge in a quest for academic certainty. This conviction helps new and inexperienced graduates to present themselves to their pupils as confident and trustworthy teachers.

## 3.7 CONCLUSION

The number of positive reports from RE students suggests that a cooperation between librarians and RE teacher educators in the process of writing assignments is a good model for learning in the induction phase of teacher education. Few students start their education and training with enough skills in academic writing to tackle the thesis required at the end of their first degree. A well-organized and -structured program in a specific subject such as RE can serve as a catalyst for individual personal and professional development. In their reports, an important part of the required exam portfolio, all the students emphasized the importance of the coherence between the teaching and learning activities, the bridge between theory and practice. All claim to have learnt a great deal from the writing process. Even those who judge the compulsory reading list of the curriculum to be relevant and interesting claim to have found in the new academic library a number of additional books to explore and many digital resources "that made me deepen my understanding of the themes I was dealing with" (quote from an RE student). Many students report that it was in the actual writing process that they realized the importance of this work for a teacher:

> As I am a very verbal person who likes to talk and to discuss my ideas with others, I have not before my RE course realized the importance of being able to express myself in writing and especially the importance of improving these skills as a teacher.
>
> **Quote from a student.**

For this student who had very little experience of academic writing, there was a long process of writing, correcting, and rewriting assignments. In this process the precepts of Grøtterud (2009, 2011) to "love and critique" helped me as the course leader to give my feedback in a helpful and constructive way. First I would tell the student what was good and interesting in the text (the love perspective) and then point to what could be improved and how this could be done (the critique perspective). To be specific and accurate in this process is very important. It motivates the student to do the work and gives them guidance in doing it. Many students underline the importance of constructive feedback as one pointed out:

> The feedback that my RE teacher gave me on my assignment was very important for my own personal development in the area of academic writing.
>
> **Quote from a student.**

As the RE course leader I found that evaluating these texts has equally been a very good learning activity for me. The on-line learning platform, *It's Learning*, creates a new connection between students and teachers. Students can ask questions and receive answers quickly. They can easily rewrite their texts in order to demonstrate the best of their knowledge and ability. For teachers, the digital space created by the learning platform develops new and closer relationships with the students. It affords an insight into the problems and questions that the students are facing in their work.

New power structures are constructed as we all participate in the development of a community of learning, sharing knowledge and experiences in the learning process. Teachers who are educated in this way in the first years of teacher education are challenged to participate in an inclusive and democratic community of learning. They are motivated to develop their capacity to model this democratic way of teaching and learning in the remaining years of teacher education, in their future work in schools and classrooms and, it is hoped, in a lifelong learning process. In their final metatexts when they look back at the study that they took part in, many of the students appreciate the quality of cooperation between them and their classmates. By sharing and evaluating their text under Grøtterud's two concepts, they were able to revise their work and improve their writing skills. They felt that their classmates helped them to do better by inspiring new reflections about their texts and suggesting how their ideas and arguments could be better phrased and composed. In their future work these students can choose to develop similar ways of work with their own learners, focusing on learner-oriented activities and a value-based pedagogy where the aim is to help each learner to do better and contribute to the construction of a democratic and sustainable school ethos. Schools that are governed by this ethos will see their work and mission as supporting a just and democratic society.

## REFERENCES

Bårnes, V., & Løkse, M. (2014). *Information literacy: How to find, evaluate and cite sources.* Oslo: Cappelen Damm Akademisk.
Brookfield, S. D. (1995). *Becoming a critically reflective teacher.* San Francisco: Jossey-Bass.
Brudal, L. (2014). *Empathic communication — The missing link.* Oslo: Gyldendal Akademisk.
Council of Europe (2008). *White paper on intercultural dialogue: Living together as equals in dignity.* Strasbourg: Council of Europe Publishing.
Council of Europe (2011). *Teacher education for change. The theory behind the Council of Europe Pestalozzi Program.* Strasbourg: Council of Europe Publishing.

Council of Europe (2012). *Intercultural competence for all — Preparing for living in a heterogeneous world: Council of Europe Pestalozzi Series, No. 2.* Strasbourg: Council of Europe Publishing.
Council of Europe (2014a). *Bookmarks — A manual for combating hate speech online through human rights education.* Strasbourg: Council of Europe Publishing.
Council of Europe (2014b). *Signposts — Policy and practice for teaching about religions and non-religious world views in intercultural education.* Strasbourg: Council of Europe Publishing.
Council of Europe (2015). *Change for education — Education for change "manifesto" Pestalozzi Program pestalozzi@coe.int.* Strasbourg: Council of Europe Publishing.
Council of Europe (2016a). *Higher education for democratic innovation. Council of Higher Education Series No. 21.* Strasbourg: Council of Europe Publishing.
Council of Europe (2016b). *Task for democracy: 60 activities attitudes, skills and knowledge.* Strasbourg: Council of Europe Publishing.
Flornes, K. (2007). An action research approach to initial teacher education in Norway (Unpublished doctoral dissertation). Birmingham, UK: The University of Birmingham.
Grøtterud, S. (2009). Love and critique in guiding student teachers. *Journal of Living Theories, 2*(1), 68—95. Available at: www.ejolts.net.
Grøtterud, S. (2011). *Developing guiding encounters in practical and didactic education — Action research in teacher educators' practice. Unpublished doctoral dissertation.* Norwegian University of Life Sciences, Department of Mathematical Sciences and Technology.
Huber, J., & Mompoint-Gaillard, P. (Eds.), (2011). *Developing intercultural competence through education. (Pestalozzi Series No 2)* Strasbourg: Council of Europe Publishing.
Hull, J. (2015). Notes on blindness [Video file]. Retrieved from: https://vimeo.com/84336261.
Imhof, M., & Picard, Ch (2009). Views on using portfolio in teacher education. *Teaching and Teacher Education, 25*(2009), 149—154.
Palmer, P. J. (1998). *The courage to teach.* San Francisco: Jossey-Bass Publisher.
Riedling, A. M. (2002). *Learning to learn: A guide to becoming information literate.* New York: Neil Schuman Publishers.
Sætre, T. P. (2007). *Bibliotekenes rolle i studentenes læringsarbeid [The role of the libraries in students' learning activities]. Learning for professional competences Skriftserien nr. 2* (pp. 145—160). HiB/BUC.
Sandos, S. (2014). *Children, ICT and ethics: A study in digital formation, using Norwegian kindergartens as case. Unpublished doctoral dissertation.* Norway: University of Trondheim.
Torras, M.-C., & Sætre, T. (2009). *Information literacy education: A process approach, Professionalising the pedagogical role of academic libraries.* Oxford: Chandos Publishing.
UNESCO. (2012). Media and information literacy curriculum for teachers. Available at http://www.unesco.org/new/en/communication-and-information/resources/publications-and-communication-materials/publications/full-list/media-and-information-literacy-curriculum-for-teachers/.
Winje, G. (2009). Åvære digital i KRL-faget. In H. Otnes (Ed.), *Åvære digital i alle fag.* Oslo: Universitetsforlaget.

# CHAPTER 4

# The School Library in Media and Information Literacy Education

S. Ingvaldsen
Sogn og Fjordane County Library, Sogn og Fjordane, Norway

## 4.1 INTRODUCTION

This chapter deals with the use of the library as a tool in pedagogical work, that is, in reading education and in the promotion of media and information literacy (MIL). To be able to use the library resources, teacher education students and library students must know what these resources consist of and how to include them in teaching. This chapter looks into what the concept MIL implies, and it emphasizes the connection between reading literacy and MIL. It argues that the school library needs to be included in curricula and annual school plans in order to play a role in daily school work.

This chapter builds on experiences from teaching school library studies at the University of Agder and at UiT, The Arctic University of Norway, and from advising on diverse projects in schools, mainly projects in the Norwegian School Library Program 2009–13. Primary and lower secondary schools in all Norwegian counties participated in the program, and 210 development projects were carried out during the project period. The program was the result of many advocacy and professional initiatives, over a long period of time, including campaigns carried out by library and reading organizations, reports at state level, and a survey of all Norwegian school libraries (Ingvaldsen, 2013). The program was designed to make sure the school library was included in reading education and in the promotion of MIL. Reading and the use of media and information sources are competencies that students need to acquire, and school libraries can serve as tools in this learning process. As such, school libraries can be essential in preparing students for further education and lifelong learning.

## 4.2 MEDIA AND INFORMATION LITERACY: A COMPLEX SET OF SKILLS

In recent decades school library research has been increasingly focused on the promotion of MIL. MIL is a complex set of skills, including information competencies that are needed through the whole learning process. These competencies are fundamental in all education. Studies show that young people need to strengthen their MIL (Alexandersson, Limberg, Lantz-Andersson, & Kylemark, 2007; Hjortsæter, 2010; Information Behaviour of the Researcher of the Future, 2008; Mangen, 2010; Roe, 2013).

In short, MIL is the ability to acknowledge one's information needs, to be able to formulate a research question, to find information, to evaluate whether this information is relevant and reliable, and to use the information efficiently and ethically while building new knowledge. Furthermore, the concept includes the ability to communicate and share this information and, lastly, to reflect upon and evaluate one's learning outcome and learning process.

Researchers have stressed that reading education and the use of information sources should be taught together (Alexandersson et al., 2007; Mangen, 2010; Rafste, 2008). It is obvious that if students do not have reading skills, they are not able to benefit from information in printed or web-based sources. In this connection it is interesting that the PISA (Program for International Student Assessment) study from 2012 defines reading literacy as "understanding, using, and reflecting on written texts, in order to achieve one's goals, to develop one's knowledge and potential, and to participate in society" (Technische Universität München, n.d.). PISA emphasizes the ability to understand and integrate texts that the students are confronted with in their everyday lives. It is not the reading speed, but the understanding and use of texts that are important in this PISA testing. The tests are developed to measure to what extent the students can:
- Retrieve texts and access them;
- Interpret and integrate texts;
- Reflect and evaluate texts.

(Technische Universität München, n.d.)

PISA includes what we have defined as elements of MIL in reading literacy. In the Norwegian School Library Program 2009—13, MIL was divided into four categories:
- Wondering about and asking questions;
- Selecting and assessing;
- Reading for comprehension;
- Creating and sharing.

The categories were designed to fit into the education of the main target groups in the program, primary and lower secondary school students. These categories are supposed to cover all aspects and phases of MIL, from encouraging curiosity and eagerness to learn to having knowledge of how to use social media in communication. The categories have similarities with Christine Bruce's seven categories of informed learning (Bruce, n.d.). Bruce divides informed learning into: using information technology for information retrieval and communication (one), finding information located in information sources (two), executing a process (three), controlling information (four), building up a personal knowledge base in a new area of interest (five), working with knowledge and personal perspectives adopted in such a way that novel insights are gained (six), and finally using information wisely for the benefit of others (seven).

The categories in the Norwegian School Library Program laid the foundation of a progression or path for teaching of MIL in schools, a plan that was tied to the Norwegian national curriculum, *Knowledge Promotion* (The Norwegian Directorate for Education and Training, 2006). The categories turned out to be useful tools for describing and systematizing the learning elements of MIL at various steps of the curriculum. Using the categories also exposed gaps in the curriculum related to MIL. One of the tasks set for the program was to propose MIL elements that would solve these deficiencies.

## 4.3 TEACHING MEDIA AND INFORMATION LITERACY

Is there a particular pedagogy that is useful in libraries and, if so, what characterizes this pedagogy? Lise Alsted Henrichsen, librarian and pedagogue at University College UCC in Copenhagen, looked into this issue in a lecture at the University of Agder, Norway (Henrichsen, 2014). She says about the joint task of teachers and librarians in library-based teaching:

> It is about being able to read one's students and to make learning objectives concrete to them as well as working towards these aims through well-chosen

*contents and well-chosen working methods — all on the background of the main aims and curriculum of the school.*

**Henrichsen (2014, p. 1, my translation).**

Henrichsen points to the fact that teachers and librarians need a common language for the pedagogical activity that takes place in the library. A challenge in this connection is that the school curriculum is divided into separate subjects, whereas the use of the school library is not a particular subject, and it should not be. On the contrary, the use of literature and information sources should be integrated into the teaching of the different subjects to make certain that students learn better.

In the school library, several professionals work together. Besides librarians, there are teachers, IT technicians, media educators, and reading advisors. This complexity makes it even more important to develop a shared pedagogical understanding among professionals. The concept of school library pedagogy is useful in order to express a common starting point for these different professional areas and competencies.

This understanding of the school library coincides with the concept of a learning center. A learning center is characterized by architecture and interiors that are designed for learning activities, and it is staffed with librarians, teachers, IT consultants, and others who all work together to promote the students' learning. Using the school library as a learning center is an approach based on constructive and sociocultural theory. We learn by gradually building on what we already know and through our interaction with others.

Henrichsen (2014) suggests that we ask a series of questions much used in pedagogical planning when discussing the particular pedagogic challenges related to MIL and the use of the school library:

- Who is to learn? (Students);
- Why do the students need to learn? (Purpose);
- What objectives are to be obtained by the learning? (Objectives);
- What is to be learned? (Contents);
- From whom are the students to learn? (The teacher/the librarian);
- Where is the learning to take place? (Learning environment);
- By means of what are the students to learn? (Learning resources).

These questions all emphasize the need to focus on the students: the school and the school library exist for them. Below each of the questions is examined from a MIL and a school library point of view.

*Who is to learn?* Today's students have an enormous amount of information available. The information society is a concept that describes this situation, with constantly new media, tools, standards, and formats. Students do not necessarily have the skills needed to cope with the information flow. According to the British report Information Behaviour of the Researcher of the Future (2008), the development of children's and young people's information literacy has not kept pace with the increased use of information technology and access to web-based information sources. The report indicates that the Google generation (youth born after 1993) has too much faith in its own abilities in information search. Children and young people often lack understanding of their own need for information, and there is a discrepancy between their assessments of their own abilities and what they actually achieve when searching for information. They do not have sufficient skills in using sources critically, and to a large extent their work is characterized by "cut and paste."

The impression of low awareness of MIL among students from several countries is supported by the OECD report *Students, Computers and Learning, Making the Connection* (2015). Based on results from PISA 2012, the report underlines the need for teachers and parents to help students become critical consumers of electronic media and Internet sources and thus enable them to make informed choices.

Blikstad-Balas has studied Norwegian students' information behavior (2013, 2016). She found that the students are very positive towards Wikipedia as a source of information. They see Wikipedia as a more relevant source than their textbooks and "consider Wikipedia's bad reputation among teachers as a far worse disadvantage than potential misinformation" (Blikstad-Balas, 2013). Even though they know that Wikipedia might convey incorrect information, this does not affect their positive attitudes towards this web-based encyclopedia. The problem is not that students use Wikipedia, in many cases an excellent source, but that they do not critically evaluate the information they find.

It seems that students need to enhance their MIL, even though they are not necessarily aware of this. To be able to make informed decisions, they must have sufficient skills in searching for and using relevant information sources.

The next question deals with the *purpose* of the school library. It is essential to keep in mind that the aim of the school library cannot be separated from the aim of the school. The library should work towards the same aim as the school does altogether. Simple as this seems, we often find examples where the school library is not integrated into the core school activities and operates as an institution of its own in the school environment. The school library must operate in alignment with the main principles of education.

The *objectives* of learning are described in the overall educational laws of a country and in guidelines and curricula for specific parts of the school system. Research shows that the school library must be included in plans for the school, both in major whole school plans and in annual subject plans, in order to find its right place in pedagogical work (Barstad, Audunson, Hjortsæter, & Østlie, 2007; Carlsten & Sjaastad, 2014; Pihl, 2011; Rafste, 2001). This is an important learning from the Norwegian School Library Program as well (Ingvaldsen, 2014). The core aims for the school library are supporting reading education and the promotion of MIL, and activities within these areas need to be planned in order to be properly integrated into the work of the school.

When it comes to the *contents*, the main point is that the MIL instruction needs to be combined with the ordinary curricular education and integrated with discipline content. Research shows that the learning outcome of MIL is improved when MIL instruction is connected to assignments that the students are to do in their ordinary subjects (Alexandersson et al., 2007; Rafste, 2008). Media and information work that is done in order to complete assignments based on problem solving, not only fact-finding, leads to the best learning outcome. The students must be involved in active learning processes which include the use of information sources. It is equally important that media and information skills are assessed properly like the work in the subjects. The learning outcome of MIL should count like other results when the students and their parents receive feedback on school work.

There are challenges combining regular curricular subjects and MIL, however. Reading education and the teaching of subjects have traditionally been the responsibility of teachers and have been researched by pedagogues and psychologists, whereas MIL has been developed within Library and Information Science. When planning for MIL education, one aim is finding a common language so that teachers and librarians can discuss these issues. In schools where such a shared understanding is achieved, different professionals can make joint efforts developing the students' MIL and integrating the library into educational activities. In the Norwegian School Library Program, this challenge was met by making it compulsory for the whole project group—the principal, the teachers, and the school librarian—to attend program courses. In order to achieve funding from the program, the participating schools had to make certain that this happened. The participants were to have knowledge of each other's professions and areas of interest, and they were to be able to discuss how to teach MIL from a common starting point.

At the same time it is necessary to identify the elements of MIL that are going to be taught at each level. Curiosity, eagerness to learn, and learning strategies are some of the central competences that schools usually wish to encourage. The Norwegian School Library Program aimed at deciding what media and information skills students were supposed to have developed at different levels of their education, and in the end what could be expected of them when entering college (Informasjonskompetanse.no, n.d.). For example, it was decided that students leaving primary school (7th grade) were to be able to formulate a research question, use encyclopedias and dictionaries, find relevant websites through advanced searches, know the main principles of copyright, and include several sources in their assignments. They were to have reading competencies that allowed them to use a variety of texts in printed and digital formats, and digital skills that provided many opportunities when deciding how to communicate what they had learnt.

## 4.4 COLLABORATION AND ANCHORING

Investigating the question of whom the students are to learn from, we need to look at the roles of those involved, especially teachers, librarians, and principals. In a classroom setting, the students will look to the blackboard or whiteboard and the teacher. The school library does not have the same center of attention. In the library the student can pay attention to any part of the room or to any of the activities going on. The library thus gives much freedom to the students. As teachers and librarians, we must decide to what extent we wish to manage the use of the library. There should be room both for structured and free activities. To develop the school library as a pedagogical resource, we must however see to it that the room is designed for learning activities.

Teachers and librarians have many ways of reaching the student in order to teach MIL and the use of the library. The decision to be an actively present professional who approaches the student is essential, which means not waiting for the student to ask, but taking the initiative to engage in the student's work. Dialogue gives the students an opportunity to formulate questions, practice discussion, and reflect upon information search and source criticism. Thus not only are information skills developed but also oral competence. Giving advice about information search or the use of sources must have the individual student's or group of students' needs as its starting point. A professional challenge is to highlight general issues related to information literacy for the students so that the knowledge they achieved working on a particular assignment may be transferred to new projects (Henrichsen, 2014). Using social media is another opportunity in the library. The students can produce films, web pages, blogs, wikis, and podcasts to document certain issues. Besides lectures in the classroom or library, digital teaching programs can be used to exercise and communicate new knowledge.

Elisabeth T. Rafste (2008) developed a tentative model for teaching MIL. This is not a strictly linear model, but it gives a picture of work tasks and progression in a school project where the students are actively engaged in carrying out an assignment. The model also proposes a division of tasks between the teacher and the school librarian. The one mentioned first is in charge of the task.

| What is to be done | Who is in charge |
| --- | --- |
| Planning a project (a problem-based assignment) | Teacher (T) and school librarian (SL) |
| Introducing the issue | T |
| Informing the students and developing the research question | T and SL |
| Approving research questions | T |
| Teaching information search | SL |
| Teaching source criticism | SL and T |
| Teaching the use of information in writing | T and SL |
| Teaching presentation techniques | T and SL |
| Assessing the students' work | T and SL |

Rafste (2008, p. 135, my translation).

In the first phase, the teacher introduces the theme and the group of students who are going to work on the project to the school librarian, and the school librarian checks out what relevant literature and electronic resources are available. If there is not much to be found, the school librarian might suggest a different topic within the curriculum. The teacher and school librarian must decide who will do what in the process, so that a clear division of roles is made. In the next phase the teacher presents the topic to the students, to make sure that all have a common understanding of it and to create motivation for the task. All students must have some knowledge of the topic to be able to formulate a research question and later to know what to look for. The students need a clear, preferably written, orientation about work methods, including the use of the school library (phase three). They are now ready to start developing their research questions, and these are approved by the teacher (phase four). In phase five the teacher and school librarian have agreed on what kinds of sources are relevant, and the students receive instruction to be familiar with these. The school librarian talks about how to plan projects like these and discusses with the students what methods may be useful.

The next step is reflecting upon how to evaluate sources (phase six). The teacher and school librarian must decide what students at a certain level need to know about source criticism. At this point concepts like relevance and authority should be discussed. Is this source useful when answering the research question? Who published the information, and is it trustworthy? Having studied the information sources, the students can conclude and express what they have learned in their own words (phase seven). Diverse writing techniques (letters, poems, reflection papers, for example) can be introduced to help students to avoid just copying the sources. In many cases it will be necessary to go through citation rules and guidelines for reference lists. The students will then work on preparing the presentation of the topic (phase eight) and, importantly, they will explain what they have learned about the research question. Lastly the students participate in evaluating their learning outcome and learning process (phase nine). The teacher and school librarian discuss their collaboration and plan how to follow up the students in further work.

To achieve a good result, the teacher and school librarian need to work closely during the project. They must have knowledge of each other's professional areas so that they can assist each other through the process. In that way both may contribute in developing the students' MIL from a situation of shallow and unsystematic googling and cut and -paste to more expert search and use of information. The model builds on the principle that the teacher and the school librarian have a joint responsibility to ensure the students' learning outcome from the project.

Collaboration between professionals working in the school library has been examined by many researchers. For example, Montiel-Overall (2008) found that five themes could be identified as essential elements of successful collaboration: school culture, positive attributes of collaborators, communication, management, and motivation. Similar elements were found by Barstad et al. (2007) in their survey of Norwegian school libraries. Reports from the schools participating in the Norwegian School Library Program concluded that collaboration between teachers and librarians was crucial in making the library an integrated part of teaching. Equally important was support from the school management. Support was needed to ensure successful projects but also to make sure that developments achieved lasted beyond the project period. The program, therefore, required that the principal be the project leader. Making space for this task was a challenge for the principals participating, but this requirement turned out to be one of the most essential criteria of success (Carlsten & Sjaastad, 2014; Ingvaldsen 2014).

Research shows that school library projects must be clearly anchored in school management and owner institutions (Barstad et al., 2007; Pihl, 2011; Rafste, 2001). When schools applied for funding from the Norwegian School Library Program, they had to send their applications through the local municipality administration. This made certain that the projects were embedded in the plans for the whole local community, and the process encouraged collaboration between project schools and public libraries (Ingvaldsen, 2012). This application path proved to be valuable, even though the evaluation of the program found that there was still a need for more communication across administrative levels (Carlsten & Sjaastad, 2014; Ingvaldsen, 2014).

Hachmann and Hansen (2011), in a Danish survey of primary and lower secondary schools, concluded that the essential drives to developing learning centers were accessibility, support from the management team, annual plans, and including students in the development process. In an action research project on primary and lower secondary schools in Norway, Nøst and Sivertsen (2014) showed that sufficient time for research and reflection, participation and engagement from the management, and provision of necessary artifacts were important elements in making the library a pedagogical tool.

## 4.5 LEARNING ENVIRONMENTS AND RESOURCES

In planning MIL instruction we should not exclude any learning area; these competencies could be taught and exercised in a variety of environments. MIL must—as we have seen above—be integrated into the ordinary curricula. To teach MIL, the school library is a useful tool, however, and we need to look at this learning environment in particular. What constitutes the school library?

First, it is important to stress that libraries today cannot be understood only as physical places. They hold both physical and digital resources, and the competencies and methods they include are equally as important as the rooms and collections.

The digital library consists of databases and web resources, organized through efficient registration systems and with appropriate search tools. The physical room is the space for the collections, with reading space and work space, as well as room for MIL and library instruction. The library is a special room in the school. It can be used for teaching, as a classroom, but it is also a room for individual work or group work, as well as for reading and contemplation. It gives opportunities for silence and for recreation.

To be useful pedagogical resources, the library's collections of books and other media must be updated and relevant both to staff and students. The teaching staff needs to contribute actively in building both physical and digital collections to make them valuable resources in their educational work. As important as acquisition is discarding material that is not relevant. Too many old books and other resources make it difficult for students and teachers to find what they need.

An efficient cataloguing system must be in place in order to find books and electronic resources. Both the physical and the digital collections must be organized according to standard cataloguing and classification principles.

The library needs to be equipped properly, with necessary IT and interiors. It must be staffed with skilled professionals who have sufficient time allocated for the activities of the library so that the students will have assistance when they need it. And lastly, there must be a library plan in place. A library without a plan is like a classroom where the teacher has no guidelines or curriculum to follow. The teaching might be excellent, but there is no guarantee that the students learn what they are supposed to.

## 4.6 INTEGRATING THE USE OF LIBRARIES IN PEDAGOGICAL WORK

Issues connected to the students' needs and to the purposes, objectives, and contents of teaching programs were all central in the Norwegian School Library Program 2009—13. So were discussions on the roles of the professionals, on learning environments, and on digital and physical resources. The 210 development projects carried out emphasized some or all of these aspects, and they all sought to systematically integrate the school library into reading education and MIL instruction. Some projects had a special focus on anchoring the library in the school management and school owner. These provided plans that served as examples for new projects. Others particularly aimed at identifying the needs of students related to MIL, and at planning courses and local curricula according to these needs. These offered useful knowledge by analyzing what skills were to be taught, what was to be the content of the teaching, and furthermore how professionals and parents could collaborate to make sure the students learned what they needed. Many schools improved learning environments by upgrading interiors, discarding books, and modernizing collections. Quite a few project schools included the public library as a resource in development work.

NIFU, the Nordic Institute for Studies in Innovation, Research and Education (Carlsten & Sjaastad, 2014) evaluated the program in 2014. The report concluded that the projects were successful but that there were still challenges when it came to the development of school libraries in Norway at the national level. There is a need both for national guidelines and for research and dissemination of knowledge between school owners and other stakeholders.

From the program management point of view, the main success factors were the requirement that the principal had to be project manager and that the entire project group had to attend compulsory courses for the school to receive project funding. Furthermore, it was essential that the school had to plan for the educational use of the library. The planning process provided support from the school management and ensured collaboration between teachers and school librarians. When principals, teachers, and librarians went to courses together, they achieved a common understanding of what needed to be done to make use of the library in MIL instruction and reading education. The courses laid the foundation for a better collaboration when the participants were back in their schools. It was interesting to observe that the school managements' expectations as to what the library could contribute often had been far too low, resulting in weak development of the school library. Enhancing the knowledge about libraries changed the situation substantially in the project schools. Three key words sum up what established success at school level: planning, cooperation, and anchoring.

As university teachers reflecting on our experiences from instructing principals, teachers, and librarians in the program and from teaching university students, some additional points stand out. We saw how important it was to build practical work on theory and research, and similarly how useful it was to include examples from daily school life in education. The school projects taught us how the libraries functioned in everyday life and how they could be better integrated in pedagogical work.

Furthermore, we experienced that close collaboration between university teachers and university librarians was crucial in the process of developing studies and program courses. For example, the university librarians provided courses in MIL for the students (i.e., the teachers, librarians, and principals from the project schools), in searching, assessing, and documenting sources and in the use of social media. Their seminars contributed substantially in enhancing the participants' competencies and prepared them for teaching MIL in schools. Talking to the teachers and librarians working in schools also gave the university librarians valuable information about what practical school work consists of. The examples from the first round of school projects helped the university librarians develop their courses for the next rounds.

## 4.7 CONCLUDING REMARKS

Summing up, from several studies, from my own university teaching, and from school projects, it was clear that there is a need to develop a shared understanding in schools about the library as a pedagogical resource. For instance, many educators in the Norwegian School Library Program seemed to have limited expectations as to what the library could contribute in school work, but they reported valuable outcomes when libraries were developed and integrated into teaching. The findings indicated that university teachers and university librarians instructing teacher education students and library students needed to include the use of school libraries in their programs. Teacher education students and library students not only need to be media and information literate themselves; they should also be able to use the library as a resource when starting their own teaching and library practice.

## REFERENCES

Alexandersson, M., Limberg, L., Lantz-Andersson, A., & Kylemark, M. (2007). *Textflytt och sökslump: Informationssökning via skolbibliotek*. Stockholm: Liber. Retrieved 15.11.15. From: http://bada.hb.se/bitstream/2320/2930/2/Textflytt.pdf.

Barstad, J., Audunson, R., Hjortsæter, E., & Østlie, B. (2007). *Skulebibliotek i Norge: Kartlegging av skulebibliotek i grunnskole og vidaregåande opplæring*. Volda: Møreforsking. (Arbeidsrapport; nr 204). Retrieved 14.11.15. From: http://www.udir.no/Upload/Rapporter/5/Skulebibliotekrapport_fullstendig.pdf?epslanguage=no.

Blikstad-Balas, M. (2013). Students' attitudes towards Wikipedia as a knowledge source in School. Retrieved 01.03.16. From: https://www.academia.edu/4464735/Students_attitudes_towards_Wikipedia_as_a_knowledge_source_in_school_-ECER_2013_Presentation.

Blikstad-Balas, M. (2016). "You get what you need": Students' attitudes towards using Wikipedia when doing school assignments. Preprint from own archive, published in Scandinavian Journal of Educational Research. Retrieved 01.03.16. From: https://www.academia.edu/15365551/_You_get_what_you_need_-_Students_attitudes_towards_using_Wikipedia_when_doing_school_assignments.

Bruce, C. (n.d.). Seven faces of information literacy in higher education. Website of Professor Christine Bruce. Retrieved 16.11.15. From: http://www.christinebruce.com.au/informed-learning/seven-faces-of-information-literacy-in-higher-education.

Carlsten, T. C., & Sjaastad, J. (2014). *Evaluering av Program for skolebibliotekutvikling 2009–2013*. Oslo: Nordisk institutt for studier av innovasjon, forskning og utdanning. NIFU-rapport 4. Retrieved 15.11.15. From: http://www.nifu.no/files/2014/03/NIFUrapport2014-4.pdf.

Hachmann, R., & Hansen, J. J. (2011). *Veje til fremtidens skolebibliotek*. Aabenraa: University College Syddanmark.

Henrichsen, L. A. (2014). *Skolebiblioteket som lærings- og danningsarena. Skolebibliotekdidaktikk - introduksjonsforelesning*. Universitetet i Agder. Retrieved 01.03.16. From: http://informasjonskompetanse.no/blog/2015/11/26/skolebiblioteket-som-laerings-og-danningsarena-forelesning-av-lise-alsted-henrichsen/.

Hjortsæter, E. (2010). *Elevers og studenters informasjonssøkeadferd*. Universitetet i Agder. Retrieved 15.03.15. From: http://skolebibliotek.uia.no/skolebibliotekressurser/informasjonskompetanse-og-kildekritikk/elevers-og-studenters-informasjonssoekeatferd.

Informasjonskompetanse.no. (n.d.). Retrieved 05.03.16. From: www.informasjonskompetanse.no.

Information Behaviour of the Researcher of the Future: A CIBER Briefing Paper. (2008). London: University College London. Retrieved 14.11.15. From: http://www.webarchive.org.uk/wayback/archive/20140614113419/http://www.jisc.ac.uk/media/documents/programmes/reppres/gg_final_keynote_11012008.pdf.

Ingvaldsen, S. (2012). Joint efforts to improve reading education: Cooperative projects between public libraries and schools in the Norwegian School Library Program. In: Proceedings of the 2012 IFLA conference. Retrieved 15.11.15. From: http://conference.ifla.org/past-wlic/2012/118-ingvaldsen-en.pdf.

Ingvaldsen, S. (2013). BSLA case study: A school library promotion campaign: "Now we see the fruits of our work and efforts": The School Library Promotion Campaign in Norway 2007–2008. In: IASL-IFLA SL joint workshops Kuala Lumpur (Malaya), August 2013. Retrieved 05.03.16. From: https://schoollibrariesontheagenda.files.wordpress.com/2013/07/bsla_iflasl-iasl_norway_case_study_2013_final.pdf.

Ingvaldsen, S. (2014). The Norwegian School Library Programme – What has been achieved? In: Paper at the 2014 IFLA conference Lyon. Retrieved 14.11.15. From: http://library.ifla.org/912/1/213-ingvaldsen-en.pdf.

Mangen, A. (2010). *Når alt finnes på nettet, hva skal vi da med skolebiblioteket? Lesing i skolebiblioteket*. Stavanger: University of Stavanger.
Montiel-Overall, P. (2008). Teacher and librarian collaboration: A qualitative study. *Library & Information Science Research, 30*(2), 145—155.
The Norwegian Directorate for Education and Training. (2006). Knowledge promotion — Kunnskapsløftet. Retrieved 15.11.15. From: http://www.udir.no/Stottemeny/English/Curriculum-in-English/_english/Knowledge-promotion---Kunnskapsloftet/.
Nøst, T. M., & Sivertsen, G. M. (2014). *Skolebiblioteket: Læringsrommet i skolens hjerte. Avhandling avlagt ved Handelshøjskolen i København og Institut for Uddannelse og Pædagogik, Universitet i Aarhus*. Aarhus: University of Aarhus.
OECD. (2015). Students, computers and learning: Making the connection. In: PISA series, published on September 15, 2015. Retrieved 05.03.16. From: http://www.oecd.org/edu/students-computers-and-learning-9789264239555-en.htm.
Pihl, J. (2011). *Multiplisitet, myndiggjøring, medborgerskap: Inkludering gjennom bruk av biblioteket som læringsarena. (Sluttrapport forsknings- og utviklingsprosjekt, Høgskolen i Oslo og Akershus)*. Oslo: University College of Oslo and Akershus.
Rafste, E. T. (2001). *Et sted å lære eller et sted å være? En case-studie av elvers bruk og opplevelse av skolebiblioteket. Unpublished doctoral dissertation*. Oslo: University of Oslo.
Rafste, E. T. (2008). Informasjonskompetanse — elevaktive og undersøkende arbeidsmetoder. In T. Hoel, E. T. Rafste, & T. P. Sætre (Eds.), *Opplevelse, oppdagelse, opplysning: Fagbok om skolebibliotek* (pp. 120—165). Oslo: Biblioteksentralen.
Roe, A. (2013). *Lesing i PISA 2012*. University of Oslo. Retrieved 14.11.15. From: http://www.udir.no/contentassets/478ff813bbdd4a6298f9a9ea646c48e3/astrid-roe.pdf.
Technische Universität München. (n.d.). Reading literacy. Retrieved 15.11.15. From: http://www.pisa.tum.de/en/domains/reading-literacy/.

# CHAPTER 5

# Teaching Faculty Collaborating With Academic Librarians: Developing Partnerships to Embed Information Literacy

T. Inzerilla
Las Positas College Library, Livermore, CA, United States

## 5.1 INTRODUCTION

Collaboration enhances student learning and provides benefits to faculty. Educational theorists have promoted collaboration among teaching faculty as a method to advance intellectual and practical student learning (Haycock, 2007; Lewis & Sincan, 2009). Some argue that when faculty members collaborate, students benefit from the collaboration by recognizing the connections across or within disciplines (Lewis & Sincan, 2009). Ideas transfer from one course to another as a result of the collaboration (Lewis & Sincan, 2009). Furthermore, students are exposed to the unique perspectives and strengths of different faculty members (Lewis & Sincan, 2009). Collaboration between faculty that involves shared goals and objectives "improves teaching and strengthens academic programs" (Lindman & Tahamont, 2006, p. 293). The experiences of collaboration help faculty to gain knowledge in each other's area of expertise and remove perceived barriers between departments (Lindman & Tahamont, 2006).

Collaboration between librarians and faculty is often accomplished in information literacy education. Many librarians argue that collaboration between faculty and librarians is imperative in teaching information literacy to students (England & Pasco, 2004). Some librarians believe building collaborative partnerships with faculty should be the key strategy for teaching information literacy to students (Zhang, 2001). From the librarians' perspective, collaboration between faculty and librarians provides students with heightened opportunities for information literacy education (Barnard, Nash, & O'Brien, 2005). This is important because information environment of respect and trust (Association of College and Research Libraries, 2011; Montiel-Overall, 2008).

#### 5.2.1.1 By Librarians
The Association of College and Research Libraries (ACRL) (2011) defines collaboration as a respectful environment involving trust, joint objectives, and goals. In the case of faculty and librarians, the members enter into collaboration with a goal of preparing students for success. Raspa and Ward (2000) define collaboration as an in-depth relationship where each of the partners contributes to making "common goals and objectives," tasks, and plans for implementation (p. 5), while cooperation involves dividing up roles and responsibilities.

#### 5.2.1.2 By Faculty
There are several forms of collaboration defined by faculty. Briggs' (2007) research found faculty members' definition of collaboration when developing curriculum to be: team teaching courses, working on course materials together, and gaining knowledge together. Team teaching is a form of collaboration and is discussed in this section because it encourages collaboration and communication among faculty members (Lewis & Sincan, 2009). Team teaching has multiple definitions including: shared assignments among two classes, cooperation where the roles of each faculty member retain control over their own material, collaboration where each faculty member equally shares the responsibility, and joint meetings of two or more courses (Ford & Gray, 2011; Lewis & Sincan, 2009; Shapiro & Dempsey, 2008; Zhou, Jinyoung, & Kerekes, 2011).

### 5.2.2 How Is Information Literacy Defined?
Information literacy is typically described as the ability to locate, evaluate, analyze, and utilize information (American Library Association Presidential Committee on Information Literacy, 1989; Association of College and Research Libraries, 2012; Chartered Institute of Library and Information Professionals, 2003). It has also been described with emphasis on its outcome "the experience of using information to learn" (Bruce, 2008, p. viii). Information literacy is commonly identified as an outcome of a community college education in the United States (Accrediting Commission for Community and Junior College: Western Association of Schools and Colleges, 2011; Middle States Commission on Higher Education, 2011; New England Association of Schools and Colleges

literacy capabilities help students to grasp concepts and to apply them in multiple disciplines (Barnard et al., 2005). Students learning information literacy are able to transfer what they learned in the academic context into their personal and professional lives (England & Pasco, 2004).

When faculty design and deliver their courses, they are engaged in a teaching social network. A teaching social network is comprised of communications that influence faculty when they design and deliver their courses. The communication may be formal (e.g., through scholarly journals and professional development activities) and informal (e.g., through personal communication) (Weedman, 1992). Attending a professional workshop or reading a professional journal on pedagogy are examples of elements that may influence the faculty member's teaching social network. When faculty are involved in team teaching, they become a part (or an element) of each other's teaching social networks. Faculty members influence each other in the way they collaborate in a team-taught course. Librarians become another element of the network when they collaborate with faculty to teach students search strategies and show them how to locate, evaluate, and analyze information related to a class assignment.

## 5.2 FACULTY COLLABORATING WITH LIBRARIANS

This chapter reports the findings of a doctoral study focused on the experience of faculty collaborating with librarians in a community college academic setting. At community colleges, librarians are considered library faculty but, for clarity in this chapter, library faculty are referred to as librarians.

The purpose of this study was to provide librarians with a new perspective from teaching faculty about their collaboration with librarians and recommendations for practice. This study explored teaching faculty's experience of collaboration in terms of motivating factors and challenges of collaboration with librarians. Two key terms were critical to this study: collaboration and information literacy.

### 5.2.1 How Is Collaboration Defined?

Collaboration involves two or more equally valuable groups or individuals entering into a well-defined relationship with mutual goals (Mattessich & Monsey, 1992). Indicators of successful faculty and librarian collaboration include developing common objectives (Chatfield, Romero, & Haworth, 2012; Holmes & Tobin, 2006; Kenedy & Monty, 2011) and creating an

Commission on Institutions of Higher Education, 2011). The governing authorities for community colleges, also known as accreditation organizations, recognize information literacy as a student learning outcome and standard that must be met, and they stress that collaboration between faculty and librarians is a strategy for meeting this standard (Saunders, 2008; Weiner, 2014). Because of the widespread acceptance of information literacy as a part of higher education, a major theme in the library and education literature has been the need for faculty and librarians to work together (Association of College and Research Libraries, 2011; Bruce, 2004; Mounce, 2010).

## 5.3 METHODOLOGY

This study used a mixed methods research approach to explore faculty members' experience of collaboration. Mixed methods research combines quantitative and qualitative data collection techniques (Teddlie & Tashakkori, 2003). Social network analysis was the quantitative method used to depict faculty's teaching social networks. Interviews were the qualitative method used to gather the motivating factors and challenges faculty experience related to collaboration with librarians. The ways in which librarians can become an integral part of the faculty's teaching networks were explored.

### 5.3.1 Participants

Las Positas College, the site of the investigation described here, is a community college located in Livermore, California. The full-time faculty members were considered to be a good participant base because there was collaboration happening at different levels.

Prior to the study beginning, the four full-time librarians at Las Positas College met to divide the faculty into three groups, related to their collaborative work with librarians. The three groups were: *collaborators, cooperators,* and *potentials. Collaborators* were those individuals who worked in conjunction with librarians when they created assignments, assessed students, and devised teaching strategies. *Cooperators* were those individuals who divided tasks between themselves and librarians, keeping a clear division of responsibilities (Montiel-Overall, 2008). The *cooperators* typically delegated the information literacy component to librarians by providing an assignment that required students to locate, evaluate, and utilize information. The librarians did not have any input into the creation of the assignment. *Potentials* (*potential collaborators*) were those individuals who did not work with librarians when developing their curriculum.

A survey was emailed individually to all 97 full-time faculty members in the college. The survey asked the faculty members to rate various elements in terms of level of influence on their pedagogy and course content. The elements ranged from family members, department faculty, college librarians, and social media to students. After the surveys were completed, 26 people were interviewed: five *collaborators*, 11 *cooperators*, and 10 *potentials*. All of the *collaborators* that completed the survey were interviewed.

### 5.3.2 Social Network Analysis

Marin and Wellman (2011) define a social network as a set of members connected by their relationships. A network member may be a person, group, or organization that has connections to other persons, groups, or organizations. Social network analysis examines the relationships between social units (elements) such as individuals or groups (Wasserman & Faust, 1994). Social network analysis is also described as research into social relationships and the results that occur because of the existence of the relationships (Tindall & Wellman, 2001). A main priority of social network analysis is to develop an understanding of how social relationships support and impede individuals in their actions (Tindall & Wellman, 2001).

### 5.3.3 Interviews

This study used semistructured interviews. Semistructured interviews provide flexibility in modifying the questions. The interviewer may change the order of the questions when they ask predefined questions to the interviewee (Fylan, 2005).

The interview questions were divided by the type of participant: *collaborator*, *cooperator*, and *potential*, with both collaborator and cooperator groups responding to the first four interview questions. The first two questions were:

1. Please provide examples of how (the element) affects you in how you teach (pedagogy/methodology, types of assignments, classroom strategies, or classroom activities) in the last 3 years
2. Please provide examples of how (the element) affects you in what you teach (content, subject matter, topics) in the last 3 years

If the interviewee had selected "extensive" or "often" for a particular element on the survey, they were also asked the following:

---

3. Please explain why (the element) is useful [in how you teach or what you teach]

---

If the interviewee had selected "some," "seldom," or "not at all" for a particular element on the survey, they were asked the following:

---

4. Please explain how (the element) can become more useful [in how you teach or what you teach]

---

Interview questions 1 and 2 were probing for a better understanding of the roles of the elements utilized within the networks. By asking the faculty member to provide examples of each element, a clearer picture was given of how the elements were used in their teaching social network. The answers to the third interview question related to why the elements were useful; it delved into the motivating factors for including the elements in the network. The answers to the fourth interview question explored how elements could become more useful and how the elements could become integral parts of the networks. By analyzing the responses for nonlibrarian elements, inferences were sought that might correlate and be applied to the librarian role.

After the first four interview questions, the *collaborators* and *cooperators* were asked the following:

---

5. Tell me why you collaborate with librarians.
6. Tell me about a time when there was a successful collaboration with librarians.
7. Tell me about a time there was an unsuccessful collaboration with librarians.
8. What are the benefits of collaborating with librarians?
9. How did you learn about collaborating with librarians? Please explain.
10. How can the library and its faculty become a more valuable resource when you are developing what you teach and how you teach it?

---

Interview questions 5 and 6 explored why librarians were included in the network and provided reasons for collaborations; interview question 7 was for finding potential barriers for collaboration that the faculty had experienced. The examples provided assured that the interviewer understood how the interviewee described collaboration with librarians. The examples were reviewed to determine whether they were examples of information literacy. Interview questions 8, 9, and 10 examined the benefits of collaborating with librarians and ways of integrating librarians into the networks. Understanding the benefits of collaborating with librarians provided the factors that motivated faculty to begin the collaboration process.

*Potentials* were only asked the following:

---
Interview question for *potentials*
11. Have you ever considered collaborating with librarians? Why or why not? Please explain.

---

This question examined the challenges that prevented collaboration with librarians and attempted to discover ways librarians could become an integral part of the networks.

## 5.4 FACULTY'S EXPERIENCE OF COLLABORATION
### 5.4.1 Influential Elements in the Teaching Social Network

According to the survey results, students, department faculty, professional development, and scholarly communications are some of the most influential elements in faculty teaching social networks (see Fig. 5.1). Students had the most influence in teaching methods and content taught for faculty. The librarians had a weak influence on faculty, but their influence may have occurred more indirectly. For example, librarians may influence faculty by influencing their students: if students commented to their faculty about the helpfulness of librarians in their research, faculty may decide to collaborate with librarians or continue the existing collaboration.

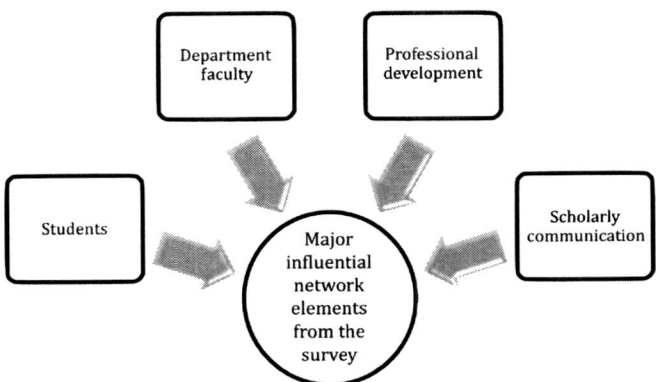

**Figure 5.1** Most influential elements in faculty's teaching social networks.

Department faculty were the second strongest influence on faculty. If librarians successfully collaborated with one member of a department, this may lead to future collaborations with other members of the same department. Professional development (conferences and workshops) was a major influence of faculty; faculty recommended that librarians provide more workshops for utilizing library resources (e.g., training on using databases). Librarians presenting at conferences where faculty attend provides a new venue for marketing the librarians' services. Scholarly communications were also a major influencer of faculty. By publishing in journals and other scholarly communications read by faculty, librarians will be utilizing another venue to reach faculty in regards to teaching methods and course content. See Fig. 5.1 to view the major elements.

### 5.4.2 Faculty's Teaching Social Networks

The survey results provided a description of the elements influencing faculty in their teaching methods and content taught. Cross and Parker (2004) discussed how social network analysis has been used to determine better ways of implementing collaboration by reviewing the current framework of collaboration. Understanding the current framework provides knowledge of where to target collaborative efforts. By reviewing the faculty's teaching social networks, librarians will be able to determine possible instructors for future collaborations. The respondents that were the most open (or influenced the most) would be good candidates. Since this is the first study to date investigating the teaching social networks of faculty through the lens of social network analysis, there is no literature against which to compare the findings.

From the survey results, librarians appeared to play a minor role in faculty's teaching social networks at Las Positas College. The study respondents considered themselves to be weakly influenced by librarians. Only one respondent in this study, a *collaborator*, saw herself as highly influenced by the librarians in her teaching methods.

The interview responses of the faculty, however, differed from their survey responses. The interviewees provided multiple examples of how the librarians influenced them in their teaching, which were not reflected in the survey responses. One *collaborator* works closely with the librarians each semester on a research assignment for his class. When he responded to the survey he indicated some affect by librarians. When he discussed the role of librarians during the interviews, he provided multiple examples of collaboration. An example was collaborating on the development and assessment of a research paper where he relied on the librarian to grade the citations.

This suggests that faculty were not fully aware of how librarians had influenced their teaching social networks. It is evident from the interviews that faculty were working with the librarians but in the survey they did not seem to fully recognize the impact of the librarians. The perception of the impact of the librarians on faculty's teaching social networks appears from this example to differ from the reality provided in the interviews. This may mean that the librarians play more of a role than they are given credit for by faculty.

The *collaborators* were the most open to being influenced by their social network elements, followed by the *cooperators* and *potentials*. One implication of this is that the focus of librarians should be on working more closely with *collaborators* and *cooperators* because they have shown openness to being influenced by other elements. A second implication is that librarians should consider carefully before focusing a lot of energy on the *potentials*. The librarians may have a difficult time changing the *potentials* into *collaborators* or *cooperators* because the evidence suggests that *potentials* were not strongly influenced by relevant elements.

Therefore, librarians should seriously consider how much time and energy they invest in *potentials* because that group is unlikely to have much interest in starting a collaborative effort. If librarians' resources and time are limited, then the amount of energy required by the librarians on trying to change the *potentials*' minds would be better spent on communication with *collaborators* and *cooperators*. If time and resources are not an issue for librarians, they could explore creative ways of engaging the *potentials*.

Many faculty members interviewed were focused on learning new ways to improve their teaching and were open to being influenced by a variety of elements, including librarians. Their goal was to provide the best possible instruction to the students. Other faculty viewed the course content they teach as their area of expertise and were not as willing to modify their content to include the librarians' information literacy content. Most libraries have a limited number of librarians to collaborate with faculty. The librarians prepared to collaborate with faculty on their teaching methods should be encouraged to do so.

### 5.4.3 Faculty's Interpretation of Collaboration

Collaboration was not defined for the participants in order to gain a better understanding of how faculty viewed collaboration. The participants revealed their interpretation of collaboration when they gave examples of how the librarians influenced their teaching. *Collaborators* and *cooperators* believed they collaborated with librarians. The interpretations of collaboration that the *collaborators* and some of the *cooperators* provided matched this study's definition; however, most of the *cooperators*' interpretations of collaboration did not. Instead the *cooperators*' interpretations of collaboration matched the definition of cooperation. *Cooperators* described collaboration as delegating the information literacy component of the course to librarians. *Potentials* and some *cooperators* felt collaboration was sending students to the library to do research, providing course reserves, and receiving updates about new library resources, which did not match the definition of collaboration used for this study.

### 5.4.4 Faculty's Interpretation of Information Literacy

As with collaboration, faculty members were not asked how they defined information literacy. The participants revealed their interpretations of information literacy when they explained why they collaborated with librarians. The responses ranged from "helping them find the information" to "it's incredibly important for students to be able to evaluate enormous amounts of information—to collect it, to understand it, and to use it" to "students are getting the broadest access to resources" to "they can provide the resource, the expertise, the materials, for example related to the area of information [literacy] and the evaluation of the credibility of information." In summary, the interpretation of information literacy revealed by the *collaborators* and *cooperators* is a set of abilities that enables the students to learn to find, evaluate, analyze, and utilize information by learning how to use the library's resources.

## 5.5 MOTIVATING FACTORS AND CHALLENGES OF COLLABORATION

### 5.5.1 Factors Motivating Faculty to Collaborate With Librarians

*Collaborators* and *cooperators* were motivated to collaborate with librarians because of the perceived benefits to their students and themselves. One of the benefits for both students and instructors was students' improved research skills which allowed them to produce better research projects (including videos, games, panels, presentations, debates, and papers). This finding is consistent with the library and education literature (Bury, 2011; Morrison, 2007). An additional benefit for the *collaborators* and *cooperators* was that they saved time by collaborating with librarians. This benefit was rarely mentioned in the literature (Ducas & Michaud-Oystryk, 2003; Simmel, 2007). Librarians should mention these benefits of collaboration when they have informal conversations about library services with faculty or when they are communicating with faculty to promote new collaborations. When faculty mention the benefits of collaborating with librarians to their peers, this may have the effect of encouraging *potentials* and *cooperators* into becoming *collaborators*, especially if faculty provide testimonials, informing their colleagues at meetings and staff development workshops.

The study participants mentioned additional motivations for collaborating with librarians. A motivating factor for collaboration was the librarians' promotion of the library and research orientations. Some areas that were promoted by librarians were "higher level journals, reference materials, an entire website [research guide] dedicated to my class, [and] the [research] orientations." The promotion of the library services to faculty encouraged them to continue collaborating. This finding was not found in the literature to date. Librarians should do their best to promote their library services to the faculty. Another motivating reason for collaboration was that faculty built strong working relationships with librarians. This finding was not found in the current literature. These relationships encourage continuous collaboration. Attending meetings, serving on committees, and attending campus events are ways to develop relationships with faculty. A third motivating factor was increasing the faculty's course content through the purchases of additional resources. Keeping faculty in mind when buying new library materials is one way for librarians to encourage collaboration. This finding has been noted in the literature (Morrison, 2007). A fourth motivating factor was reducing library anxiety in students and was also found in the literature (Bury, 2011; Manuel, Beck, & Molloy, 2005).

There were benefits of collaborating with the other elements that could be applied to collaborating with librarians. The benefits were sharing ideas, learning from different perspectives, and mitigating the teaching in isolation feelings that come from working alone. These benefits were not mentioned in the library and education literature. When promoting collaboration with noncollaborating faculty, these benefits should be mentioned to encourage participation in working with librarians.

Another important area to recognize is that librarians' personal characteristics are a motivating factor for collaboration. Helpfulness, supportiveness, and trustworthiness were characteristics appreciated by the *collaborators* and *cooperators* and encouraged them to keep collaborating with librarians. Another characteristic was librarians' knowledge or expertise. Expertise was a motivating factor in the library literature (Manuel et al., 2005). Creativity is another motivating characteristic that could be applied to librarians from the network elements. Librarians should not hesitate in being creative in their teaching approach when working with faculty. Practitioners should make sure they are displaying these characteristics to the faculty. Having, displaying, and communicating these characteristics will open up collaboration opportunities with faculty.

There were motivations for collaborating with librarians mentioned in the literature that did not surface during the interviews for this study. These included:

- Students develop critical thinking skills due to learning how to research (Manuel et al., 2005);
- Students become lifelong learners (Manuel et al., 2005; Morrison, 2007);
- Students learn and improve essential research skills and become independent researchers (Morrison, 2007);
- Students expand communication abilities by encouraged psychological growth (Manuel, Molloy, & Beck, 2003); and
- Students become better prepared for employment opportunities (Morrison, 2007).

However, this might be explained by the fact that the studies cited above were conducted at 4-year colleges, while this study was conducted at a community college.

One other motivating reason not mentioned in this current study was reducing students' dependence on internet websites for their research (Morrison, 2007). However, during informal conversations with librarians, both full-time and part-time faculty in the community college have mentioned that they want students to use more than websites in their research.

This study has indicated there are strong reasons for faculty collaborating with librarians and if this knowledge is utilized well by practitioners, it will make a significant impact in their collaboration efforts.

## 5.5.2 Challenges Preventing Collaboration With Librarians

Challenges of collaboration between faculty and librarians have been extensively discussed in library and education literature (Bury, 2011; Macdonald, 2009; Manuel et al., 2005; McGuinness, 2006).

This study revealed the challenges for faculty of collaborating with librarians. The biggest challenge of collaborating with librarians for *collaborators* and *cooperators* was librarians' inefficient use of teaching techniques during research orientations. A reaction of the faculty and feedback from the students indicated content provided by the librarian was not understandable and the students were not engaged during the sessions. The literature concurs with this challenge (Feldman & Sciammarella, 2000; Manuel et al., 2005). One way to address this challenge is for a higher emphasis on pedagogical training for librarians, either through initial professional education or professional development. Such development opportunities might include formal coursework, conferences, or workshops that discuss ways of teaching that are interactive and effective. A surprising challenge that came during the interviews about the other elements was that faculty members blamed themselves for not initiating contact with others.

There were challenges of collaborating with librarians for the *potentials* that agreed with the literature. Some *potentials* did not see a reason to collaborate with librarians because they did not have research assignments in their classes (Leckie & Fullerton, 1999). The students' writing skills were not at a proficiency level, and it made reading their research papers too difficult and time-consuming. Without research projects, it is highly unlikely these *potentials* will collaborate with librarians. There could be a creative effort made by librarians to engage the *potentials* in unique ways by offering to provide assistance in creating research projects. Lack of time for collaboration was an additional challenge for *potentials* (Ducas & Michaud-Oystryk, 2003). As discussed in the motivating factors section, librarians need to inform the instructors that collaborating with librarians can be a time saver. One *potential* felt it was too difficult to schedule a research orientation (Leckie & Fullerton, 1999). Librarians should address this challenge when marketing their research orientations by offering to work with faculty in scheduling their orientations.

One of the challenges for faculty of collaborating with librarians is faculty culture (Badke, 2010; McGuinness, 2006; Morrison, 2007). Hardesty (1995) suggests that academic freedom is a reason instructors will not collaborate with librarians. However, the only time an interviewee mentioned academic freedom was in regards to administration and how they did not want them involved in the content: "It's a violation of my academic freedom for [administration] to get involved in what I teach."

The literature also suggests that challenges to collaborating with librarians arise from faculty's perceptions of their students: students would approach either faculty and librarians when they needed assistance with their research (Feldman & Sciammarella, 2000; Leckie & Fullerton, 1999), students already know how to do research (Ducas & Michaud-Oystryk, 2003; Feldman & Sciammarella, 2000; Leckie & Fullerton, 1999), or they ask other students for help (McGuinness, 2006). Challenges related to faculty's instruction were also cited: faculty stated that they could not insert an information literacy component into their already full course (Feldman & Sciammarella, 2000; Leckie & Fullerton, 1999), they preferred to do their own information literacy instruction (Ducas & Michaud-Oystryk, 2003; Gonzales, 2001), or they felt librarians did not have enough subject knowledge (Ducas & Michaud-Oystryk, 2003; Manuel et al., 2005). These findings, however, were not mentioned by the faculty in this study.

Recognizing the challenges of collaboration with librarians will enable librarians to create ways to eliminate the challenges.

## 5.6 WAYS LIBRARIANS CAN BECOME EMBEDDED IN FACULTY'S CLASS INSTRUCTION

Through previous research literature, faculty have provided suggestions for librarians to become more embedded in faculty's class instruction. See Fig. 5.2 for these suggestions.

This study revealed further ways for librarians to become more useful to faculty's teaching social networks. *Collaborators* and *cooperators* suggested librarians connect faculty to discipline-specific resources. These connections may be made through email or by going to department meetings and giving demonstrations of databases related to their discipline. This would be an excellent way for librarians to build rapport and establish future collaborations. An additional suggestion was going to the instructor's classroom instead of requiring the instructors to come to the library. Librarians should market the research orientations as both taught in the library and in the faculty member's classroom. This may

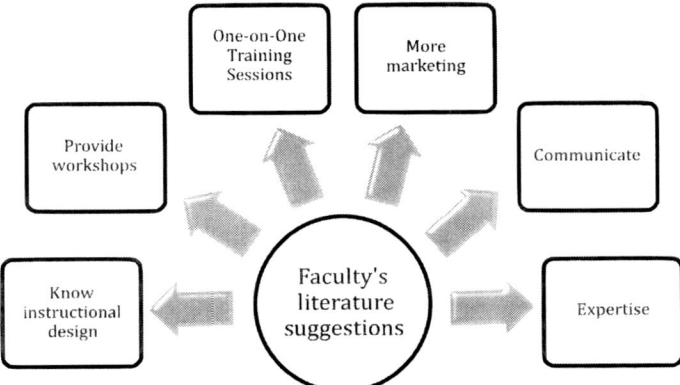

**Figure 5.2** Faculty's literature suggestions for making librarians become more useful to teaching social networks.

lead to more opportunities and show more flexibility on the part of the librarians. The *potentials* suggested librarians develop preresearch assignments for their students. Talking with a faculty member about his or her course and offering to create a preresearch assignment may be the beginning of a new collaboration. All three groups suggested the librarians provide additional access to resources. Finding funding to purchase additional materials might be seen to be outside the responsibility of librarians but seeking new grant opportunities and trying to establish new ways of funding will be beneficial in promoting collaborations.

Faculty suggested that the librarians should initiate discussions about teaching with faculty. Faculty wants more conversations about teaching (e.g., pedagogy, course content, and engaging students). Conversing about teaching, assuming the librarian has a background in teaching or pedagogy, is a way to share ideas and get to know the instructors better, which will lead to future collaborations. Gonzales (2001) also mentions encouraging more teaching conversations with faculty who do not collaborate with librarians.

A way for librarians to be more integral in faculty's teaching social networks is to provide additional training for the faculty. One form of training is making available more workshops on how to use the library's resources, and this is also noted in the literature (McGuinness, 2006). Professional development, which includes campus workshops, was strongly influential for the survey responders. If librarians offered professional development opportunities by providing campus workshops or providing sessions at conferences that their faculty attends, they have a higher probability of being more influential to faculty. Another form of training is one-on-one training sessions or one-on-one consultations. Offering personal opportunities to meet exclusively provides another form of outreach and collaboration.

Discovering the ways *collaborators* and *cooperators* learned about collaborating with librarians may also suggest new ways of targeting faculty for future collaborations. One way of learning about collaboration for participating faculty was through their colleagues. Instructors that already work with librarians could be encouraged to invite their colleagues to collaborate with librarians. Another way is by informal interactions with librarians. This suggests librarians need to prioritize interacting more with faculty by going to committee meetings, campus events, walking around the campus, or having impromptu discussions with faculty members as they walk through the library. The third popular way of learning about collaborating with librarians was through new faculty orientations. This suggests contacting administration or whoever sets up the new faculty orientations and requesting that the library be placed on the schedule.

In Fig. 5.3 faculty's suggestions from this study are highlighted, indicating strategies for librarians to become more influential in faculty's teaching social networks.

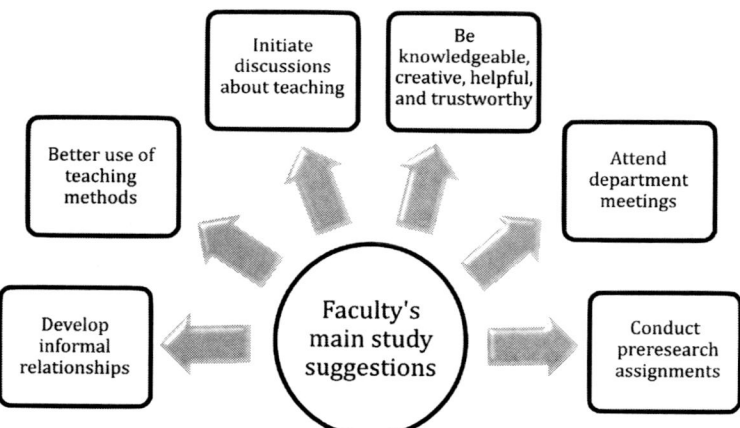

**Figure 5.3** Faculty's suggestions for having librarians become more useful to teaching social networks.

## 5.7 RECOMMENDATIONS FOR PRACTICE

This study provided ideas and suggestions from faculty related to how librarians can become more integral to teaching social networks. This section provides recommendations for future practice. The recommendations that are particularly suited to a workshop style professional development opportunity are indicated with (Workshop). They are divided into five categories described below.

*Develop common definitions for collaboration and information literacy*:
- Develop an understanding of faculty member's interpretation of collaboration before the collaborative process begins. This will provide a basis of understanding between both parties and open the lines of communication.
- Build services in information literacy from the point of view of the faculty instead of from the librarian perspective.
- Create a short survey for the faculty that currently collaborate (or cooperate) with librarians and ask them to indicate the reasons they collaborate. There should be a short list including students' research projects improved, faculty saved time by collaborating with librarians, and a few more choices pertinent to the college or school. The respondents that indicated they save time by collaborating with librarians should be asked if they could be used in promotional materials distributed to the rest of faculty. This is a great way to promote new collaboration opportunities with faculty. (Workshop)
- Librarians and faculty should review the definitions of information literacy and move from a skills-based interpretation to a learning process or social and information practice.

*Create more opportunities for communicating with faculty*:
- Increase marketing efforts of the library services available. Some library services that should be promoted are research orientations, library databases, reference books, and research guides dedicated to their classes. More opportunities for collaboration will occur if faculty is made aware of the library services available to them. (Workshop)
- Develop a strong rapport with faculty by attending college functions and joining college committees that discuss teaching concerns. Examples of such committees are curriculum, program review, or student learning outcomes. Interacting more with faculty will lead to new collaboration opportunities.

- Make opportunities to communicate more with faculty about teaching. An example of an opportunity may be volunteering to evaluate a faculty member's class. Communicating more about teaching will lead to more discussions that may lead to additional collaborative opportunities.
- Engage faculty in unique ways of marketing when they do not collaborate with librarians by encouraging the addition of research projects.

*Expand opportunities for training faculty:*

- Develop more training sessions for faculty, such as one-on-one interactions and group workshops on using the library's resources. (Workshop)
- As a part of staff development opportunities for faculty, provide more opportunities to engage in reflection on their teaching. (Workshop)
- Informing faculty of how to use social media in their courses may be one way of making librarians more influential to faculty's teaching. (Workshop)

*Encourage pedagogical training:*

- Enroll in classes or go to professional development workshops to learn how to become a better instructor. Make sure the classes cover dynamic teaching techniques and new ways of interactive teaching and engaging students. This would improve the effectiveness of the research orientations. (Workshop)
- Schools that offer library and information science programs should provide more classes in pedagogy and how to teach.

*Discover additional funding for the library:*

- Seek grant opportunities that will provide additional funding to the library. (Workshop)

## 5.8 CONCLUSION

Many interesting ideas for collaborating with faculty emerged from this study. Some of the ideas had already started being implemented at my community college. For example, one suggestion from the teaching faculty was to make the library more visible to the college. This was accomplished by ensuring one librarian was a member of each of the main committees including but not limited to the curriculum, student learning outcomes, distance education, technology, and facilities committees. A committee added was academic senate because of opportunities for visibility with faculty. I have had the opportunity to implement several of the suggestions at my community college. One example is developing more conversations with faculty about research. For several years, my community college did not have flex days, but in February 2016, there will be a roundtable discussion about research with teaching faculty. I am hopeful there will be a discussion of how faculty implement research in their courses and ways the librarians can assist faculty with their efforts. All of the librarians do as much collaboration with their faculty colleagues as possible, including team teaching, creating learning communities, and developing and assessing assignments together. The amount of collaboration by the librarians increased after I received a new role as head librarian. This collaboration has gone well since the teaching faculty initiated the collaboration. For example, a psychology instructor approached me to team teach the research portion of his course. This has been a successful collaboration. Another suggestion that has started being implemented is to market the library services to faculty. Beginning in Spring 2015, an email was sent at the beginning of the semester promoting library services such as research orientations. This marketing effort has increased the number of orientations requested and completed by the librarians. A key learning from the study was not to dwell on the noncollaborating faculty, since this study suggests that great efforts will be needed to change the situation. Whenever possible the librarians are encouraged to attend workshops related to pedagogy. This has helped enhance their classes and research workshops.

Some suggestions from the study have not been currently implemented at my college. For example, teaching faculty have been instructing faculty how to use social media in their courses through workshops. Another suggestion not implemented is seeking grant opportunities. There has not been enough time to focus on this endeavor but requests for funding are included in program reviews for the library. At times, administration grants the library's requests. A third suggestion not implemented was reviewing the definitions of information literacy with faculty and moving the definition to a learning process. There has not been enough time to accomplish this goal. One of my goals as head librarian is to attempt to implement all of the suggestions from my study. Even though some of the goals have not been accomplished at my college, the feedback received from both the librarians and teaching faculty has been very positive about the collaborative experience and both would like to continue collaborating together to teach the students information literacy.

## ACKNOWLEDGMENTS

This chapter is based on Tina Inzerilla's thesis: *Community College Faculty's Teaching Social Networks and Their Implications for Librarians* (2012) located at: http://eprints.qut.edu.au/62700/. Ethical clearance (Ethics Number 0900000604) was obtained from Queensland University of Technology. Permission was also received from Las Positas College. I would like to thank Dr. Christine Bruce for her encouragement and assistance with this chapter.

## REFERENCES

Accrediting Commission for Community and Junior College: Western Association of Schools and Colleges. (2011). Accreditation standards. Retreived from: http://www.accjc.org/eligibility-requirements-standards/2002-standards-of-accreditation/.

American Library Association Presidential Committee on Information Literacy. (1989). Final report. Retreived from: http://www.ala.org/ala/mgrps/divs/acrl/publications/whitepapers/presidential.cfm.

Association of College and Research Libraries. (2011). Collaborating with teaching faculty. Retreived 07.10.08. Retreived from: http://www.ala.org/acrl/issues/infolit/resources/collaboration/collaboration#faculty.

Association of College and Research Libraries. (2012). Introduction to information literacy. Retreived from: http://www.ala.org/ala/mgrps/divs/acrl/issues/infolit/overview/intro/index.cfm.

Badke, W. (2010). Why information literacy is invisible. *Communications in Information Literacy*, 4(2), 129−141.

Barnard, A., Nash, R., & O'Brien, M. (2005). Information literacy: Developing lifelong skills through nursing education. *Journal of Nursing Education*, 44(11), 505−510.

Briggs, C. L. (2007). Curriculum collaboration: A key to continuous program renewal. *The Journal of Higher Education*, 78(6), 676−711.

Bruce, C. (2004). Information literacy as a catalyst for educational change: A background paper. In: Paper presented at the the 3rd international lifelong learning conference, Yeppoon, Queensland. Retreived from: http://eprints.qut.edu.au/4977/1/4977_1.pdf.

Bruce, C. (2008). *Informed learning*. Chicago, IL: Association of College and Research Libraries.

Bury, S. (2011). Faculty attitudes, perceptions and experiences of information literacy: A study across multiple disciplines at York University, Canada. *Journal of Information Literacy*, 5(1), 45−64.

Chartered Institute of Library and Information Professionals. (2003). Information literacy: Definition. Retreived from: http://www.cilip.org.uk/get-involved/advocacy/learning/information-literacy/Pages/definition.aspx.

Chatfield, A. J., Romero, R. M., & Haworth, I. S. (2012). Information intervention in the pharmaceutical sciences. *Medical Reference Services Quarterly*, 31(2), 188−201. Available from: http://dx.doi.org/10.1080/02763869.2012.670593.

Cross, R., & Parker, A. (2004). *The hidden power of social networks: Understanding how work really gets done in organizations*. Boston: Harvard Business School Press.

Ducas, A. M., & Michaud-Oystryk, N. (2003). Toward a new enterprise: Capitalizing on the faculty/librarian partnership. *At the University of Manitoba*, 64(1), 55−74.

England, L. E., & Pasco, R. J. (2004). Information literacy − Making it real! *Community & Junior College Libraries*, 12(3), 67−72.

Feldman, D., & Sciammarella, S. (2000). Both sides of the looking glass: Librarian and teaching faculty perceptions of librarianship at six community colleges. *College & Research Libraries*, 61(6), 491−498.

Ford, J., & Gray, L. (2011). Team teaching on a shoestring budget. In: Honors in practice — Online archive. Paper 137. Retrieved from: http://digitalcommons.unl.edu/nchchip/137.
Fylan, F. (2005). Semi-structured interviewing. In J. Miles, & P. Gilbert (Eds.), *A handbook of research methods for clinical and health psychology* (pp. 65–78). New York: Oxford University Press.
Gonzales, R. (2001). Opinions and experiences of university faculty regarding library research instruction: Results of a web-based survey at the University of Southern Colorado. *Research Strategies*, 18(3), 191–201. Available from: http://dx.doi.org/10.1016/s0734-3310(02)00090-3.
Hardesty, L. (1995). Faculty culture and bibliographic instruction: An exploratory analysis. *Library Trends*, 44(2), 339–367.
Haycock, K. (2007). Collaboration: Critical success factors for student learning. *School Libraries Worldwide*, 13(1), 25–35.
Holmes, A., & Tobin, E. (2006). Motivation through collaboration at St. George's School of Montreal. *School Libraries in Canada (17108535)*, 25(2), 40–43.
Kenedy, R., & Monty, V. (2011). Faculty-librarian collaboration and the development of critical skills through dynamic purposeful learning. *Libri: International Journal of Libraries & Information Services*, 61(2), 116–124. Available from: http://dx.doi.org/10.1515/libr.2011.010.
Leckie, G. J., & Fullerton, A. (1999). Information literacy in science and engineering undergraduate education: Faculty attitudes and pedagogical practices. *College & Research Libraries*, 60(1), 9–29.
Lewis, K. O., & Sincan, M. (2009). International co-teaching of medical informatics for training-the-trainers in content and distance education. *Journal of Asynchronous Learning Networks*, 13(2), 33–47.
Lindman, J., & Tahamont, M. (2006). Transforming selves, transforming courses: Faculty and staff development and the construction of interdisciplinary diversity courses. *Innovative Higher Education*, 30(4), 289–304.
Macdonald, K. (2009). Out of the boot camp and into the chrysalis: A reflective practice case study. *Australian Library Journal*, 58(1), 17–27.
Manuel, K., Beck, S. E., & Molloy, M. (2005). An ethnographic study of attitudes influencing faculty collaboration in library instruction. *Reference Librarian*, 43(89/90), 139–161.
Manuel, K., Molloy, M., & Beck, S. (2003). What faculty want: A study of attitudes influencing faculty collaboration in library instruction. In: Paper presented at the ACRL eleventh national conference, Charlotte, North Carolina. http://www.ala.org/acrl/files/conferences/pdf/manuel.pdf.
Marin, A., & Wellman, B. (2011). Social network analysis: An introduction. *The Sage handbook of social network analysis* (pp. 11–25). Los Angeles, CA: Sage.
Mattessich, P. W., & Monsey, B. R. (1992). *Collaboration: What makes it work: A review of research literature on factors influencing successful collaboration*. St. Paul, MN: Amherst H. Wilder Foundation.
McGuinness, C. (2006). What faculty think-exploring the barriers to information literacy development in undergraduate education. *The Journal of Academic Librarianship*, 32(6), 573–582.
Middle States Commission on Higher Education. (2011). Characteristics of excellence in higher education: Eligibility requirements and standards for accreditation. Retrieved from: http://www.msche.org/publications/CHX-2011-WEB.pdf.
Montiel-Overall, P. (2008). Teacher and librarian collaboration: A qualitative study. *Library & Information Science Research*, 30(2), 145–155.
Morrison, L. M. (2007). Faculty motivations: An exploratory study of motivational factors of faculty to assist with students' research skills development. *Partnership: The Canadian Journal of Library & Information Practice & Research*, 2(2), 1–20.

Mounce, M. (2010). Working together: Academic librarians and faculty collaborating to improve students' information literacy skills: A literature review 2000–2009. *The Reference Librarian, 51*(4), 300–320.

New England Association of Schools and Colleges Commission on Institutions of Higher Education. (2011). Standards for accreditation. Retreived from: http://cihe.neasc.org/standards_policies/standards/standards_html_version/.

Raspa, D., & Ward, D. (2000). Listening for collaboration: Faculty and librarians working together. In D. Raspa, & D. Ward (Eds.), *The collaborative imperative: Librarians and faculty working together in the information universe* (pp. 1–18). Chicago, IL: American Library Association.

Saunders, L. (2008). Perspectives on accreditation and information literacy as reflected in the literature of library and information science. *The Journal of Academic Librarianship, 34*(4), 305–313.

Shapiro, E. J., & Dempsey, C. J. (2008). Conflict resolution in team teaching: A case study in interdisciplinary teaching. *College Teaching, 56*(3), 157–162.

Simmel, L. (2007). Building your value story and business case: Observations from a marketing faculty and (former) librarian perspective. *College & Research Libraries News, 68*(2), 88–91.

Teddlie, C., & Tashakkori, A. (2003). Major issues and controversies in the use of mixed methods in the social and behavioral sciences. In A. Tashakkori, & C. Teddlie (Eds.), *Handbook of mixed methods in social & behavioral research* (pp. 3–50). Thousand Oaks: Sage.

Tindall, D. B., & Wellman, B. (2001). Canada as social structure: Social network analysis and Canadian sociology. *Canadian Journal of Sociology/Cahiers canadiens de sociologie, 26*(3), 265–308.

Wasserman, S., & Faust, K. (1994). *Social network analysis: Methods and applications.* New York: Cambridge University Press.

Weedman, J. (1992). Informal and formal channels in boundary-spanning communication. *Journal of the American Society for Information Science, 43*(3), 257–267.

Weiner, S. A. (2014). Who teaches information literacy competencies? Report of a study of faculty. *College Teaching, 62*(1), 5–12.

Zhang, W. (2001). Building partnerships in liberal arts education: Library team teaching. *Reference Services Review, 29*, 141–149.

Zhou, G., Jinyoung, K., & Kerekes, J. (2011). Collaborative teaching of an integrated methods course. *International Electronic Journal of Elementary Education, 3*(2), 123–138.

CHAPTER 6

# Teaching Source Criticism to Students in Higher Education: A Practical Approach

**H. Johannessen**
Agder University Library, Bergen, Norway

## 6.1 INTRODUCTION

The quantity of available information increases every day, and therefore the ability to handle and evaluate this information is becoming more and more vital. The skills enabling this are often referred to as information literacy. Since its origin in 1974, this term has shifted meaning several times, but the basics remain that an information-literate person should be able to identify a need for information, search for relevant sources, critically evaluate these sources, and use them in an ethical manner.

This chapter deals with source criticism and the teaching of this. This chapter is limited to teaching undergraduates, as this is a well-known challenge. Undergraduates are less likely to be experienced in their subject and less likely to have a full overview of the literature in their field. They need skills that are not too subject-specific in order to get started with evaluating sources. While postgraduates have experience in and knowledge about evaluating sources, undergraduates can (and should) be taught some basic skills. These are skills that can be identified and taught. As librarians, we must not only *be* information literates, but also *educators* of these skills. In this chapter, an introduction to how librarians can teach source criticism and evaluation of sources will be given. But first, an introduction to what role source criticism plays in information literacy and student learning is given.

## 6.2 INFORMATION LITERACY AND DIFFERENT LEARNING THEORIES

With the changing information environment comes new expectations and challenges for librarians. Librarians are not only behind a desk answering questions, but also need to be in the academic environment as educators. More library instruction is needed in the information society, and the instruction must be of high quality, and not left to chance. A pedagogical approach is vital to get the message across (Mokhtar, Majid, & Foo, 2008, p. 101). To be able to teach, one must also know how students learn. Learning theories are helpful to make a systematic approach to teaching and to express the desired learning outcome for the students attending library courses. Learning theories will also help structure your teaching. A reflection upon applied pedagogical approaches must be made by librarians to further effect and develop their teaching (Elmborg, 2006).

Library instruction is often subject to a one-shot instruction session. This makes it difficult to thoroughly assess the long-term benefits of library instruction and information literacy skills for the students. The "Google Generation" has grown up using the Internet as a source of information. They are trained in accessing information quickly and easily, but finding academic literature of high quality is quite different from finding a quick definition or a link to a webpage.

There are many strategies to finding quality information sources, and teaching this is one of the librarians' most important tasks. Information literacy learning theories are often divided into three main groups: the behavioristic, the phenomenographic, and the sociocultural perspective.

## 6.2.1 The Behavioristic View of Information Literacy

A behavioristic view of information literacy emphasizes generic, measurable skills. The behavioristic approach is not subject-specific, but a set of generic skills that are believed to be transferrable to other subjects. The focus is on creating, elaborating, and passing on text-based information. It can also be viewed as critical thinking and communication skills. The behavioristic view is the most basic understanding of information literacy, which involves the teaching and learning of measurable skills on how to handle information.

This view of information literacy is reflected in the Information Literacy Competency Standards for Higher Education developed by the Association of College and Research Libraries (ACRL) of the American Library Association (2000):

> *Information literacy forms the basis for lifelong learning. It is common to all disciplines, to all learning environments, and to all levels of education. It enables learners to master content and extend their investigations, become more self-directed,*

and assume greater control over their own learning. An information-literate individual is able to:
- Determine the extent of information needed;
- Access the needed information effectively and efficiently;
- Evaluate information and its sources critically;
- Incorporate selected information into one's knowledge base;
- Use information effectively to accomplish a specific purpose;
- Understand the economic, legal, and social issues surrounding the use of information, and access and use information ethically and legally.

This is an example of how a behavioristic view of information literacy presents concrete generic skills, which can be measured and transferred to other contexts. ACRL has more recently developed a Framework for Information Literacy in Higher Education that reflects more phemenological and sociocultural perspectives on information literacy. This is illustrated in the new definition where information literacy is described as a "set of integrated abilities encompassing the reflective discovery of information, the understanding of how information is produced and valued, and the use of information in creating new knowledge and participating ethically in communities of learning" (Association of College & Research Libraries, 2015, p. 3).

## 6.2.2 The Phenomenographic View on Information Literacy

Phenomenography is concerned with how people understand, perceive, and make use of different phenomena. A phenomenographical understanding states that information literacy is not transferrable and generic, but situated. In this case, information literacy is understood as something that changes with content, situation, and context as this is experienced by the information seeker. Phenomenography sets out to *understand* information literacy, as behaviorism wants to measure it. Phenomenography insists that information literacy is situated and not to be understood in the same way in different settings.

The consequence this has for teaching is that each university subject must be offered library instruction suited to their academic context. Students studying engineering will have different information needs than language students, and each may need a library instruction session suited for their information needs.

## 6.2.3 The Sociocultural Perspective

The sociocultural view on information literacy states that information literacy is something developed in community with others. Developing information literacy skills is concerned with how information is found and used in a given social situation. The sociocultural perspective states that the training of information literacy skills is deeply situated. Individuals develop information literacy in social interaction in a context where these skills are considered to be of value. People are socialized into a context and situated within this context (Lloyd, 2012).

A sociocultural view suggests that it is more rational to talk about *information literacies* rather than information literacy. A sociocultural view lifts the information literacies out of the library and academic world and into the given context, whether it is kindergarten or working life.

Annemaree Lloyd has published extensively on information literacy and her article from 2007 *Learning to put out the red stuff*, is one of the most well-known approaches to a sociocultural view of information literacy skills. The article concerns itself with how information literacy skills are used in a work environment. In this article, firefighters' skills and ability to learn through a social setting are the focus. Not all skills can be learnt in a formal education setting. Some are better understood through observing other, more experienced co-workers. This is also a good way of accessing tacit knowledge. Tacit knowledge is an important part of workplace knowledge, but is difficult to pass on to new co-workers. This type of learning can best be achieved in a "community of practice" or a group of people who engage in collective learning (Wenger, 2001).

Every community has its idea of information literacy skills. Information literacy in a sociocultural context is understanding the norms of the community and what skills are important to master. For example, librarians will need competencies in knowledge organization such as classification and cataloguing, while firefighters will need different information relevant for their work. Learning what is important is often done through experience and community with other, more experienced co-workers. "Once knowledge has been captured and codified, knowledge needs to be shared and disseminated throughout the organization" (Dalkir, 2011, p. 142). In other words, we learn from each other, when developing a community of practice.

In summary, information literacy is often viewed as *either* generic or situated. Generic skills are transferrable, meaning that a student attending a library instruction session will learn skills that he or she can use in other subjects. Situated skills are attached to a certain environment, and cannot be transferred to other contexts. Information literacy is most likely the result of a combination of the two. A basic understanding of searching and information structure will be transferrable, but information needs are often situated in the subject at hand and will affect the choice of databases and search engines. Source criticism is connected to knowledge and practice in a field, which can only truly be achieved through experience. However, students need to start somewhere to gain this experience. Studies have proved that students who are given only limited guidance in source criticism will chose more questionable sources (Halverson, Siegel, & Freyermuth, 2010, p. 619).

## 6.3 ONE-SHOT INSTRUCTION, SUBJECT-SPECIFIC ADJUSTMENTS, AND MEDIA AND INFORMATION LITERACY

Good skills in source criticism require experience and acquaintance with one's own subject and experience in selecting adequate sources. This is a challenge for librarians, who are often expected to teach classes one lesson at a time (one-shot instruction). It forces the librarian to focus on some general and transferrable skills that enable the students to select and evaluate adequate sources. However, these skills should be linked to the subject at hand to make them more understandable. General information is difficult to learn if it is not related to concrete phenomena (Bloom, 1956). Christine Bruce has also made a similar conclusion:

> If we are presenting students with apparently technical information practices, such as retrieval and organization, we need to ensure that we are encouraging them to maintain a focus on what they are learning about their field or project along the way. We also need to talk with them about using their learning tasks, and the information practices intrinsic to them, as learning opportunities.
> 
> **Bruce (2008, p. 64)**

Students often do not see the need for information literacy skills before they are acquired in a concrete assignment (Daland, 2015). Massis (2011) stresses that library–faculty collaboration produces the most effective information literacy instruction. Collaboration between the library and the faculty increases the perceived value of library instruction for students because it will be understood as more integrated with the subject. Cooperation with professors will also help include MIL instruction in the teaching of subjects. If there is an understanding of the importance of library instruction from the professor and this is included in the semester plan together with other subjects, it is more likely that students will see the importance.

"Media and Information Literacy is a recently developed pedagogical approach that takes into consideration the new cultures emerging from the

Information Society" (UNAOC, n.d.). Media and information literacy (MIL) could serve as a systematic approach to incorporate information literacy into education and teaching of subjects. UNESCO has provided an MIL curriculum for teachers stating that "Basically, the curriculum framework explains a structure for developing a programme of study about media and information literacy and through various levels of engagement with media and information channels. The competencies identify the knowledge, skills and attitude that the curriculum is expected to develop" (UNESCO, 2011, p. 21). The MIL curriculum further focuses on educating teachers to teach information literacy to their students themselves. This may be a fruitful way of integrating information literacy into the curriculum. It will also promote sociocultural learning of information literacy (IL), where IL skills are integrated deeply into the subject at hand.

### 6.3.1 This Chapter's Delimitations

The sociocultural approach suggests that there is no one right way to teach or conduct source criticism. Source criticism is highly complex and must be addressed as such. Sources have different usage and different value in different subjects. While a newspaper article from 1952 is of little interest to an engineer, it could be vital to a historian. Some subjects may reject older information sources, while other subjects value them greatly. It is important to be aware of these differences when teaching source criticism. Because this is a chapter for librarians teaching source criticism in many different subjects, a behavioristic approach to information literacy will be used. It is important for the librarian to be familiar with the subject the students are studying in order to adjust these transferrable skills into more subject-specific skills, and to further a sociocultural way of teaching information literacy.

## 6.4 TEACHING SOURCE CRITICISM AS PART OF INFORMATION LITERACY: WHEN DOES ONE START TO EVALUATE?

Source criticism is often considered to be most important when evaluating one's results after the searching process. However, source criticism is also important even before one starts the actual searching process. Choice of search terms affects the search result and consequently what sources one is left with to evaluate. An example of this could be searching for information about economy and recession. If search terms like "bankruptcy" or "financial crisis" are used, it will affect the result list, and perhaps not give a balanced result. Using more neutral search words, words that describe an event or subject objectively using subject terms, will provide a more balanced result list.

Selecting search terms requires that the students are critical of themselves and that they confront their prejudices and prior understandings and beliefs when searching for and obtaining information. One will often have a tendency to look for information that confirms one's prior understandings. This is an instinctive behavior, which needs to be identified and addressed in order to change it. In teaching information literacy, the librarian must emphasize that, in much academic writing, more than one side of a subject needs to be accentuated. The discussion in an academic assignment is often based on using contradicting sources of information.

Studies have shown that "students are aware of and frustrated by their own problems with selecting and evaluating information" (Head, 2008, p. 437). It also takes intellectual confidence and a mature understanding of disciplinary and methodological literatures to be able to say that one has enough literature (Green, 2010). This confidence is not built in a day, and often students do not know where to start. Kuhlthau describes this as the "task initiation stage" (Kuhlthau, 2004), where the student is experiencing a high level of stress and uncertainty. People also tend to avoid hard tasks that entail thinking and challenging oneself (Hattie & Yates, 2014). However, when students are in the "focus formulation stage," Kuhlthau (2004) suggests that they are ready to receive information from library instruction. They now know what they need, and they are ready to do the work they are required to do. This has also been confirmed in a study published in 2015 where two different groups of students were given the same library instruction, and then assessed as to their level of satisfaction. The group working on their bachelor assignment was more motivated than the group participating without a specific assignment, and thus more satisfied with the library instruction (Daland, 2015).

## 6.5 TEACHING STUDENTS TO SEARCH FOR AND ASSESS SOURCES

It is important to stress that the searching process is an organic process that takes time and that there is no one correct answer on how to do this. The students need to practice in order to master the art of searching, and they should begin their critical thinking as early as before and during the search process.

*Practical tips when teaching students to search for information:*
- Explain the complexity of source criticism, even in the information searching process;
- Advise students to use neutral search terms;
- Advise students to try to find sources that contradict each other, even if that makes the job more difficult for them.

## 6.6 THE FIVE WS APPROACH TO SOURCE CRITICISM: EVALUATING SOURCES AND ASSESSING SEARCH RESULTS

Although source criticism starts in the searching process, the later evaluating of the sources found is still the most important part of assessing sources. Different sources must be evaluated in different ways, but there are some common denominators that can systemize the process and make it easier.

One example is the five Ws approach to source criticism, which will be introduced below. "The Five Ws" was found outside the library literature and is considered to be easier than the more established CRAAP and CRITIC methods (Radom & Gammons, 2014).

It must be said that checklist approaches like this have been critiqued, because they aim to simplify a complex process, and perhaps make it seem easier than it is. This is mainly because checklists may provide a false security, but also because they may provide "false negatives" for sources like Wikipedia, which does not have listed authors, which is thought to be untrustworthy, but still has been proven in some cases to be as trustworthy as other sources (Ostenson, 2014).

However, checklists are a good starting point, as long as the students are informed of the complexity of source criticism, and that this is a mere overview and support for them to get started.

### 6.6.1 A Suggested Approach to Teach Students Source Criticism

Encouraging students to keep a sceptical approach to sources is always a good starting point, and a way to do this is to approach the source with the "five Ws":
- Who;
- What;
- When;
- Where;
- Why.

#### 6.6.1.1 Who
When considering a source, the author must be evaluated. Has this person got a relevant education? Has (s)he published other texts in the same field of research? Does a university, or another serious institution employ this person? Has this person's writings been discussed in the media? A researcher who has been frequently cited may either be an important and respected academic, or (s)he may be highly controversial. A Google search will provide some information about the author, but it is also a good idea to search for this person in a library database to see who has cited them, and how their research is referred to.

#### 6.6.1.2 What
What is this text? Is it a blog post or an academic article? Is it an official website? Identifying whether the source has been through an official publishing process with peer review, or if it is posted online on a blog or private webpage gives an indicator of the source quality. The peer reviewing process will be presented later in this chapter.

#### 6.6.1.3 When
When was the text published? In most cases, the newest publications are the most relevant, but when working with a subject set further back in time, publications in relation to that date will be more relevant. Changes in legislation will also play a role in considering the publication date and the publication's relevance.

#### 6.6.1.4 Where
Where has the text been published? Is the publisher reliable, and is there a peer review procedure? Is the publisher reputable? Is this an academic publisher, or a popular science channel? Again, the peer reviewing process of the publisher will play an important part of the assessment.

#### 6.6.1.5 Why
Students need to consider why different texts have been written. Not all texts aim to inform and educate. Some texts want to sell a product, an idea, or a conviction. Students must consider the motives of the author. Examples to show this can be comparing web pages from a corporate company or a political party to a scientific article. However, it is important to inform students that almost no text is completely objective. There will always be an author with an interest

or a motive behind every text. This is one reason why it is important to find contradicting sources.

After considering the five Ws, students must consider the language and tone in which the text is written (the "How"). A precise and objective language will make the text more serious, and thus seem more academic. One can also detect whether subject terms are used in the text. However, if the text serves as a primary source, a normative language, speaking for a political conviction might give the information needed. It cannot be considered to be an academic text if the statements are not well grounded. One of the most important attributes of evaluating a source as adequate and academic is whether it is peer reviewed or not.

## 6.7 USING THE FIVE WS IN LIBRARY INSTRUCTION

These interrogations will help students get started with source criticism. But each source must be considered in regard to its purpose in the making of a new text. One can, of course, use a newspaper article to highlight current society's understanding of a phenomenon, but this cannot be considered to be the truth, or even an objective, well-argued picture of the truth. Most newspapers have a political standpoint, and this will color their version of the truth.

The five Ws may be a simplifying way of explaining source criticism, but it still provides the librarian with an outline to approach bibliographical data that is important when assessing sources. Many students believe that sources located in the library bookshelves or the library database will provide quality information, but the library contains sources for many purposes and audiences. An old religious book from the 1800s will be a good source for hermeneutical analysis of changes in religious texts, but it will be a poor source of information to current religious practice.

## 6.8 THE CITATION COMPASS: SOURCE CRITICISM ONLINE

The Citation Compass is a website for ethical use of sources and source criticism (Citation Compass, n.d.). This webpage is meant for use as a work of reference, but also for librarians teaching use of sources and source criticism. The examples provided serve as illustrations in teaching, and the students are able to find the same examples later when they are working alone.

One of the main focuses of the Citation Compass has been to make frequently asked questions accessible. In the development work of the Citation Compass, librarians working towards different subjects have been involved from Agder University Library, Stavanger University Library, and Telemark University College. The purpose of the webpage is not to be an inexhaustible resource, but a starting point for reflection and discussion that can be adjusted to teaching source criticism in several subjects. Some examples of things that should be considered when critically evaluating sources have been made available in a lucid overview with the possibility of more in-depth information on each box (see Fig. 6.1).

A source's value is not constant in time or in circumstance. Still, some types of sources are useful in most academic assignments. A selection of commonly used sources and their value and limitations is presented below.

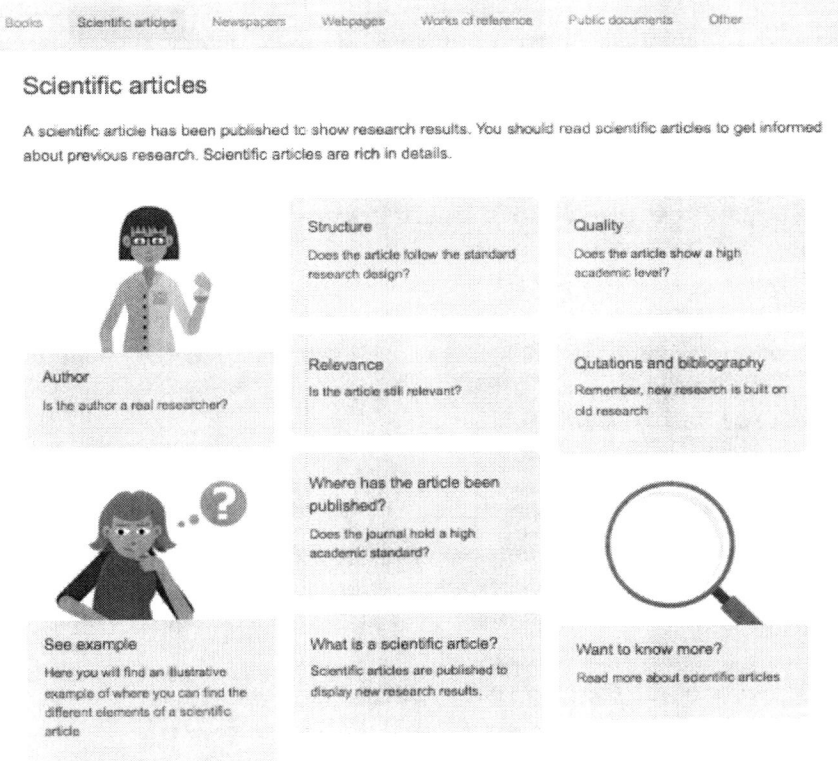

**Figure 6.1** The Citation Compass.

## 6.9 ACADEMIC TEXTS

When writing an academic text, the best sources are usually other academic texts, but these also come in different varieties. Students should be able to identify characteristics of academic texts, such as a complete bibliography, figures and tables, academic language, and an accredited publication channel. Students should also be familiar with the publishing process, such as the peer reviewing process.

### 6.9.1 Peer Reviewed?

The peer reviewing process is a quality mark for academic texts. When an academic has conducted research and written an article or book, this text is sent to a suitable publisher. An editor receives the text and considers if the quality is high enough to send out to the reviewers. If so, the text is anonymously sent to a fixed number of reviewers educated in the same research field as the author. If the text is considered adequate, the text is published. However, in most cases the reviewers have some concerns regarding the text that need to be addressed before the text is published. The author will receive these comments and is given the opportunity to make the requested changes and then get published. The peer review process makes sure the research methodology is sound and that the text provides new research knowledge to the field. It also ensures that the text is trustworthy. This is a quality stamp for academic text, but still one needs to be critical of the content. Another peer-reviewed article may contradict the conclusion given. Emphasizing this element in teaching students source criticism will provide them with important knowledge to better understand the academic publishing process and how quality is ensured.

### 6.9.2 Key Elements in an Academic Text

In an academic text, there are some key elements that should be present as a minimum. Students attending library instruction should be presented by the following key elements that an academic text should contain:
- Citations and a bibliography;
- Structure of the text, for example, IMRAD structure;
- Presenting new insight and making one's own voice heard;
- Transparent methodologies and approaches;
- Information about the publisher.

Academic texts could be scientific articles, anthologies, or books published by a reliable publisher. The text should be written by an author who is an educated professional, and it should contain a bibliography. Scientific articles are often built on the IMRAD-structure, which stands for Introduction, Methodology, Research, And Discussion. This is a well-known structure for scientific articles that makes it easy to identify the different parts of the text. It is also a good introduction in library instruction to show how an academic article is built, because it is based on definite elements that can be easily identified.

## 6.10 THE INTERNET AS A SOURCE FOR INFORMATION

The problem of the availability of information is the enormous amounts of it. While academic texts earlier were located in books or journals, now both academic texts and texts like blogposts are located on the Internet. This makes quality evaluation harder. The Internet is not an entirely good or bad provider of information. Each source must be evaluated. The Internet also hosts newspapers and other sources, and cannot be considered as a general source of information.

## 6.11 EVALUATING NONACADEMIC SOURCES AND IDENTIFYING THEIR SOURCE VALUE

Students should be taught the difference between an academic text and other sources. However, one cannot rule out the value of nonacademic sources completely. Nonacademic sources, such as newspaper articles, can be an important source for current or historical events.

Different sources have different areas of application and therefore different value or use.

If one is looking for new objective knowledge, a research article is the best choice. However, if the goal is to find opinions on a past issue, older newspapers will be a better choice.

Newspaper articles are not peer-reviewed and are not academic. They can nonetheless be of use in an academic setting, because they will actualize the subject at hand. Newspapers are, however, often politically bound, and this is important to consider when using a newspaper article. This source should not be considered as totally factual. It will be useful to hand out a newspaper in source criticism instruction lessons so that the students may see for themselves how this text differs from an academic source.

Students may want to use other student's assignments as source or even a template for their work. Student assignments have been subject to guidance from a university teacher, and they have some academic quality. It is not recommended to use a student assignment as the main basis of a new student assignment, but it has value as one of many sources. Using student assignments in the process of writing an academic text will provide value, but in the final product other sources should have been consulted and cited.

Interviews and other personal communications are considered to be primary sources, but they must be considered as an interpretation of the occurrence at hand. Though these sources may provide an impression of what has happened, it is important to be aware that they are always interpretations from the persons telling the story.

## 6.12 TEACHING COMPLEX SKILLS IN ONE-SHOT INSTRUCTION

In order to teach complex skills in just one hour, the skills must be broken down into manageable parts. The five Ws approach is one way of doing this. It must be clear that they are not being provided with a solution, but rather a set of skills to reflect upon the sources available to them to make an appropriate selection. Some things, like peer-reviewed articles, are easy to identify but other non-academic texts are harder to judge. Handing out or showing different types of sources will be a good way of exemplifying how texts differ, and showing how they might support each other.

The field of source criticism is a complex one. This is mostly because the use of the different sources in different settings makes it impossible to rule something completely out. This is also subject to differences in subjects. While health sciences have their set criteria of what is considered to be a scientific, and therefore suitable, source for students, the history subject has great focus on the fact that all sources are an interpretation of what really happened. Students need to consider what an academic text is, in each setting, and also what type of sources can be used to *create* an academic text.

## 6.13 SOURCE CONSCIOUSNESS

Being conscious of which sources to use starts in the process of searching for sources. The search terms selected and the databases or search engines

chosen will affect the result list. This is tacit knowledge and must be emphasized explicitly for students attending library instruction. Here are some focus points for teaching students to make educated source choices:
- Choose neutral search terms

    Loaded search terms will affect the result list and therefore what information the students are able to assess and use. This also means being critical of oneself and what type of information one is looking for. Academic works need to consider sources that both strengthen and weaken the author's hypothesis.
- Chose academic databases over search engines

    Library databases have a higher quality of metadata and of sources available in them. An Internet search will provide millions of results, with little possibility to limit the results. Google Scholar is a good alternative to basic web searches, because it covers academic sources.
- Identifying characteristics of academic sources

    When locating academic sources, some characteristics should be found to approve the source. Checklists are not unfailing, but will provide a good introduction to important characteristics.

Students must master not only how to create an appropriate reference list; they must learn how to avoid twisting the meaning of the text at hand. Being critical of oneself and what sources should be included and which should be disregarded is a difficult task. Most people will look for information confirming their hypothesis. This relates to both source criticism and ethical use of sources. An academic text sets out to display several sides of a problem and discusses the different approaches perspectives.

## 6.14 CONCLUSIONS

Information literacy is a complex area and, if we accept the sociocultural model (Lloyd, 2007), this is a skill, or a set of skills that must be taught and learnt in different ways depending on the context we are in. It is difficult to say that someone is information-literate or information-illiterate, but there are skills that will make information retrieval easier and that also make selection of relevant sources and ethical use of these sources more understandable. Learning those skills also helps students to deal with the frustration that is a part of the information-seeking process, as Kuhlthau (2004) discovered in her research.

Source criticism is becoming increasingly important as the Internet is making more and more information available at everybody's fingertips.

A systematic approach to teaching information literacy is important for librarians. In this chapter an introduction to different learning theories and approaches to information has been given. The described skills are generic, and it is expected that librarians make adjustments in order to make their teaching more subject-specific. The sociocultural approach to information literacy states that information literacy skills are situated and developed in community with others. Being part of an academic or professional community will affect what information literacy skills are considered important and valuable.

Source criticism is important from early in the search process, because one needs to be critical of oneself and what search terms are used. Students must be made aware that most people will search for information confirming their initial beliefs, and that this should be avoided in academic research and writing.

Different sources have different value depending on their setting. While academic, peer-reviewed texts are the most commonly used sources in student assignments, interviews, student works, and newspapers also have their place in certain settings. Students will need guidance and help to get started developing their source criticism skills.

Librarians have an important role to play, not only in educating students in source criticism, but also in educating their teachers. Educating teachers and incorporating information literacy into the curriculum is a good approach to ensure that students learn essential information literacy skills.

## REFERENCES

American Library Association. (2000). Information literacy defined. Retrieved 31.03.15. From: http://www.ala.org/acrl/standards/informationliteracycompetency#ildef.

Association of College & Research Libraries (2015). *Framework for information literacy for higher education*. Association of College & Research Libraries (ACRL). Retrieved 21.01.16. From: http://www.ala.org/acrl/standards/ilframework.

Bloom, B. (1956). *Taxonomy of educational objectives: The classification of educational goals*. New York: McKay.

Bruce, C. (2008). *Informed learning*. Chicago: Association of College and Research Libraries.

Citation Compass. (n.d.). Retrieved 01.03.16. From: http://kildekompasset.no/english.

Daland, H. T. (2015). Just in case, just in time, or just don't bother? Assessment of one-shot library instruction with follow-up workshops. *LIBER Quarterly, 24*(3), 125−139.

Dalkir, K. (2011). *Knowledge management in theory and practice* (2nd ed.). Cambridge, MA, USA: MIT Press.

Elmborg, J. (2006). Critical information literacy: Implications for instructional practice. *The Journal of Academic Librarianship, 32*(2), 192−199.

Green, R. (2010). Information illiteracy: Examining our assumptions. *The Journal of Academic Librarianship, 36*(4), 313–319.

Halverson, K. L., Siegel, M. A., & Freyermuth, S. K. (2010). Non-science majors' critical evaluation of websites in a biotechnology course. *Journal of Science Education and Technology, 19*(6), 612–620.

Hattie, J., & Yates, G. C. (2014). *Visible learning and the science of how we learn*. Abingdon: Routledge.

Head, A. J. (2008). Information literacy from the trenches: How do humanities and social science majors conduct academic research? *College & Research Libraries, 69*(5), 427–446.

Kuhlthau, C. (2004). *Seeking meaning: A process approach to library and information services* (2nd ed.). Westport, CT: Libraries Unlimited.

Lloyd, A. (2007). Learning to put out the red stuff: Becoming information literate through discursive practice. *Learning, 77*(2).

Lloyd, A. (2012). Information literacy as a socially enacted practice: Sensitising themes for an emerging perspective of people-in-practice. *Journal of Documentation, 68*(6), 772–783.

Massis, B. E. (2011). Information literacy instruction in the library: Now more than ever. *New Library World, 112*(5/6), 274–277.

Mokhtar, I. A., Majid, S., & Foo, S. (2008). Teaching information literacy through learning styles: The application of Gardner's multiple intelligences. *Journal of Librarianship and Information Science, 40*(2), 93–109.

Radom, R., & Gammons, R. W. (2014). Teaching information evaluation with the five Ws. *Reference & User Services Quarterly, 53*(4), 334–347.

Ostenson, J. (2014). Reconsidering the checklist in teaching Internet source criticism. *Portal: Libraries and the Academy, 14*(1), 33–50.

UNAOC. (n.d.). About media and education literacy.Retrieved 01.03.16. From: http://milunesco.unaoc.org/about-media-and-education-literacy/.

UNESCO. (2011). Media and information literacy curriculum for teachers. Retrieved 01.03.16. From: http://unesdoc.unesco.org/images/0019/001929/192971e.pdf.

Wenger, E. (2001). Communities of practice. In N. J. S. B. Baltes (Ed.), *International encyclopedia of the social & behavioral sciences* (pp. 2339–2342). Oxford: Pergamon. Retrieved from: http://www.sciencedirect.com/science/article/pii/B0080430767003612.

# CHAPTER 7

# Staff Development Programs on Teaching Skills and Curriculum Integration of Academic and Information Literacy at the University of Auckland

L. Wang and S. Cook
University of Auckland, Auckland, New Zealand

## 7.1 INTRODUCTION

The role of the academic library is evolving. Rather than simply providing information, academic libraries are gradually becoming more integrated into teaching, learning, and research activities in higher education (Bell, Dempsey, & Fister, 2015; Gillingham, 2013). In this changing environment, librarians' roles are also evolving from one of service providers to one of educators (Lippincott, 2015; Moselen & Wang, 2014).

Librarians are heavily involved in teaching through the provision of drop-in or course-related workshops. They also have the opportunity to work as partners with faculty teaching staff, to "become resources for innovative teaching and learning activities, and guide students as they create new types of content for their course assignments" (Lippincott, 2015, para. 5). Librarians at many institutions are now focusing on collaborating with faculty to develop thoughtful assignments by integrating information literacy (IL) into the curriculum and to ensure assignment tasks are constructively aligned with learning outcomes. They also collaborate with faculty to scaffold the development of students' research, critical thinking, and communication skills as required by the graduate profile attributes (Jaguszewski & Williams, 2013). They work with faculty to develop new assignments that both connect to the disciplinary content and encourage students to apply academic and information literacy (AIL) capabilities.

These new roles require librarians to be equipped with an understanding of student-centered learning pedagogy, curriculum design, and curriculum integration knowledge and skills. As Delaney and Bates (2015) have pointed out, librarians will need to be able to articulate learning outcomes and have an understanding of curriculum structure and curricular design in order to develop IL-related activities and deliver learning outcomes.

However, Lippincott (2015) has pointed out that many academic librarians have had no formal teacher training to prepare them for these new roles. Traditional one-off, face-to-face teaching sessions can vary in quality depending on prior training librarians have received. They "neither scale well nor do they necessarily address broader curricular goals" (Jaguszewski & Williams, 2013, p. 6).

Like faculty teaching staff, librarians do not necessarily have the necessary pedagogical background to advise on effective teaching methods and assignments related to IL and even when they do, "faculty do not necessarily recognize or value that expertise" (Jaguszewski & Williams, 2013, p. 7). A research project conducted at the University of Auckland indicated that many of its librarians felt they lacked pedagogic knowledge and skills in curriculum design and integration of IL (Moselen & Wang, 2014).

In order to equip our librarians and learning advisers with knowledge of student-centered teaching pedagogy, curriculum integration, and curriculum design, the University of Auckland Libraries and Learning Services has developed intensive staff development programs. In this chapter we explain two IL-related programs: the *Presenter Training* program and the *Curriculum Integration of Academic and Information Literacy* program.

## 7.2 THE UNIVERSITY OF AUCKLAND LIBRARIES LEARNING SERVICES

The University of Auckland is the largest and highest-ranked university in New Zealand, ranked 82nd worldwide in the 2015/16 QS World University Rankings (QS, 2016). There are eight faculties covering most disciplines with nearly 41,000 students studying at both undergraduate and postgraduate levels. There are over 7000 academic and professional staff.

In 2013, Student Learning Services was merged into the Library. In order to reflect this change, the Library was renamed as Libraries and Learning Services (LLS). LLS has a total of 248 FTE staff, including 91 professionally qualified librarians and 17 learning or language advisers.

The *Presenter Training* program is targeted towards all LLS staff who are involved in teaching or presenting. Participants normally include subject librarians, learning advisers, learning support service librarians, client services librarians, and library assistants. The *Presenter Training* program focuses on teaching skills underpinned by sociocultural learning theories (Vygotsky, 1981). It is aimed at teaching librarians and learning advisers and has been running for 10 years. There are four 3.5-hour face-to-face modules in this program.

The *Curriculum Integration of Academic and Information Literacy* staff development program is for subject librarians, learning advisers, and learning support services librarians who collaborate with faculty teaching staff on curriculum design and the integration of AIL. The Curriculum Integration of Academic and Information Literacy program focuses on curriculum and curriculum integration theories and practice underpinned by a curriculum integration model (Wang, 2013), Bloom's taxonomy (Bloom, Engelhart, Furst, Hill, & Krathwohl, 1956), and the Research and Development Framework (Willison & O'Regan, 2007). It is targeted at subject librarians, learning support services librarians, and learning advisers who are collaborating with faculty teaching staff to provide AIL education. It has been running for 3 years. There are five blended modules in this program.

## 7.3 PRESENTER TRAINING PROGRAM

In the 1990s and early 2000s, subject librarians at the University were offering drop-in workshops and course-related tutorials for students on information seeking and evaluation. However, at this stage they had no formal training in lesson plan design, student-centered learning pedagogies, or learning theories.

In 2002, subject librarians were given the opportunity to attend teaching workshops offered by the University's Centre for Professional Development (CPD). These workshops later evolved into the Presenter Training program for LLS staff involved in teaching and presenting.

Since 2005, the Presenter Training program has continued to be refined and developed. The program is run in collaboration with CLeaR (CPD was replaced by CLeaR—Centre for Learning and Research in Higher Education). It has gained an excellent reputation amongst LLS staff, and all new librarians and learning advisers, as well as library assistants who will be involved in teaching, are now required to complete the program. The program is offered once or twice a year, and participants include a mix of 10—12 experienced and novice presenters.

The Presenter Training program focuses on a student-centered learning approach underpinned by sociocultural learning theories (Vygotsky, 1981). Sociocultural theories describe learning and development as being embedded within social events and occurring as learners interact with other people, objects, and events in a collaborative environment (Vygotsky, 1978). Based on sociocultural theories, human cognitive development cannot be separated from the social, cultural, and historical contexts from which such development emerges (Johnson, 2009). This social and cultural engagement is mediated by culturally constructed tools such as language, learning objects, online resources, books, symbols, etc., that create uniquely human forms of higher-level thinking (Wang, Bruce, & Hughes, 2011).

Sociocultural theories embody a learner-centered approach and this approach is emphasized throughout the training program. Sociocultural theories help participants in the program understand how students learn. The program emphasizes the importance of creating an interactive learning environment in order to engage students and create a community of learners. A community of learners can be defined as a group of learners who "share values and beliefs and who actively engage in learning from one another—learners from teachers, teachers from learners, and learners from learners" (The Charles A. Dana Center, n.d., para. 2).

The four 3.5-hour face-to-face modules in the program cover the following topics:

1. Sociocultural theories and application in practice;
2. Teaching practice and peer discussion;
3. Designing great tutorials/presentation;
4. Teaching practice and video reflection.

## 7.3.1 Module 1: Overview of Learning Theories

Module 1 focuses on sociocultural learning theories, student-centered learning, student engagement, and establishing a community of learners. It also includes presentation style, such as verbal and nonverbal communication and body language.

In the second half of the module, three experienced LLS staff offer short presentations to demonstrate different teaching styles and approaches. Each presentation is followed by a group discussion. Participants share what they learnt from the demonstration, making linkages back to the previous discussions on learning theories and presentation style. The experienced presenters also share some of their teaching tips. As a follow up to the module, a summary of the group discussion and teaching tips is provided to all participants.

### 7.3.2 Module 2: Teaching Practices

Module 2 provides an opportunity for each participant to practice what they learnt from Module 1. Each participant gives a short 8–10-minute presentation on any LLS topic. This is followed by group discussion where each participant is expected to share feedback on the presentation (what worked well, plus any suggestions for improvement). This enables the formation of a community of learners as participants learn from each other as well as reflecting on their own teaching practice. After Module 2, a summary of the group discussion and feedback is sent to each individual participant. This enables further reflection for future teaching purposes.

### 7.3.3 Module 3: Designing Tutorials/Presentations

Module 3 focuses on how to design great tutorials and presentations. It explores different learning styles and how students learn; how to make teaching more engaging and effective; creating a lesson plan; and designing and structuring a teaching session with a student-centered learning approach. This session is facilitated by a staff member from the CLeaR team.

### 7.3.4 Module 4: Teaching Practice and Reflection

In the final module, participants are given the opportunity to put into practice what they have learnt during the program. This session is facilitated by a CLeaR staff member. Each participant presents a 5–10-minute presentation session whilst being videoed. This is followed by group discussion and feedback. The discussion includes the opportunity for each presenter to comment on what he/she has learnt and any areas they feel need improving. The facilitator also provides feedback. By this stage the program participants have formed a community of learners where sharing in this "safe" space provides a valuable learning opportunity for everyone.

After Module 4, the group discussion and self-reflection comments are summarized and sent to each participant. Participants are encouraged to keep the summary and refer back to the feedback to inform their teaching practice. The video presentations are also made available for individuals to view.

Throughout the program, student-centered learning activities are incorporated into each module in order to demonstrate student engagement to the participants. Sample activities include: ice-breaker activities; group discussion; pair discussion; learning by doing; think-pair-share; post-it notes; problem-based learning; use of props; and the demonstrate-reflect-discuss model.

Over the past ten years, over 100 librarians and learning advisers have completed the Presenter Training program. Feedback has been extremely positive. For example, one participant (a new librarian) commented that he felt very well-supported and guided throughout the program and was much more confident to start teaching. Another participant commented that despite having over 20 years teaching experience she still gained new knowledge. Several participants commented that although presenting in front of their peers was challenging it was extremely valuable.

In this program, we see the zone of proximal development (ZPD) in action. ZPD is defined by Vygotsky (1978) as "the distance between the actual developmental level as determined by independent problem solving and the level of potential development as determined through problem solving under adult guidance or in collaboration with more capable peers" (p. 86). Through the formation of a community of learners in the program, novice participants can learn much from more experienced participants. At the same time, the program enables more experienced participants to reflect on their teaching and share useful teaching tips with others. At the end of the program, several participants indicated that they would like to continue sharing teaching tips and experiences with their fellow program participants—suggesting that once a community of learners is formed it can become self-sustaining beyond the confines of an organized program.

As a result of the program, LLS staff are able to gain the necessary confidence and pedagogical understanding to ensure their teaching sessions are based on a student-centered learning approach.

## 7.4 CURRICULUM INTEGRATION OF ACADEMIC AND INFORMATION LITERACY PROGRAM

This program has been running since 2011 and was reported on in 2014 (Moselen & Wang). The program was significantly revised in 2014 due to Student Learning Services merging with the Library in 2013. The revised program was expanded from focusing purely on IL to focusing on academic *and* information literacy. This section will focus on the revised program.

The original program focused on IL and was based on Wang's curriculum integration model (Wang, 2013) and Bloom's taxonomy (Bloom et al., 1956). The revised program not only extends the focus from IL to AIL but also shifts the focus from skillset to both skillset *and* mindset. To do this, the program takes a transformative approach, incorporating reflective questions which encourage higher-order thinking on the part of participants. They are asked to reflect on their role within broader University teaching and learning activities, for example, curriculum review. This encourages them to extend their thinking beyond the perspective of a librarian to thinking like an academic. As Gillingham (2013) has pointed out, it is not just about the new skills librarians need to have, but also about the mindset which empowers them to collaborate with faculty teaching staff.

Other learning frameworks such as RSDF (Research Skills Development Framework) (Willison & O'Regan, 2007) and constructive alignment approach were also included in the revised program.

The revised program still contains five modules as shown in the table below.

| Module | Delivery method | Time |
| --- | --- | --- |
| Module 1. Academic and information literacy (AIL) for learning | Discussion with own team | 2−3 h reading and assignment + 1-h team discussion |
| Module 2. Understanding your faculty curriculum | Face-to-face | 3−4 h reading and assignment + 3.5-h class |
| Module 3. Collaboration: The foundation of AIL integration | Face-to-face | 3−4 h reading and assignment + 3-h class |
| Module 4. Design and integration of AIL into the curriculum | Face-to-face | 4−5 h reading and assignment + 3.5-h class |
| Module 5. Measuring the impact of AIL integration | Online + face-to-face informal discussion | 4−5 h reading and online assignments |

### 7.4.1 Module 1: AIL for Learning

Module 1 is designed for participants to gain a deeper understanding of the concept of AIL, the importance of AIL, and the roles that librarians and learning advisers can play in supporting student learning. Participants are required to discuss module 1 assignment questions with their team, based on the readings provided. The readings include the new ACRL information literacy framework, publications about AIL and AIL-related University documents, for example, University Graduate Profiles and University Teaching and Learning Plan.

### 7.4.2 Module 2: Understanding Your Faculty Curriculum

Module 2 is the first time participants meet together face-to-face. The session includes a summary of module 1 assignments and an icebreaker activity to enable subject librarians and learning advisers to get to know each other.

The module covers an overview of curricula in higher education; the different levels of curricula; the process of creating and changing courses at the University; and how to analyze an academic program curriculum to identify potential academic courses for AIL integration. A particular feature of the module is a series of videos in which faculty teaching staff discuss when they would change their course content, assignments, and assessment tasks. They also elaborate on the processes they follow in order to make these changes, as well as the curricular approval process involved when setting up a new course in a department or faculty.

Module 2 includes one assignment with two key tasks. One of these tasks asks participants to find out if approval is needed to change academic course content, assignments, and assessment tasks within a faculty.

The other task requires that they collaborate with learning advisers/subject librarians and a learning support services librarian with expertise in IL and learning design. They need to select an academic program, determine who the course lecturers are for each course, and then identify at least one potential course in each year of a degree that would be suitable for AIL integration.

### 7.4.3 Module 3. Collaboration: The Foundation of AIL Integration

This module is designed for participants to understand the nature of collaboration; the importance of collaboration in AIL integration; how to collaborate with others at the University; and who they can collaborate with in terms of AIL integration. The module includes a series of videos in which faculty teaching staff talk about their workload requirements and the balance between their teaching, research, and service contributions. Faculty teaching staff also comment on how they established relationships and collaborated with subject librarians and learning advisers.

A special feature of this module is the inclusion of a panel discussion in which a course coordinator, subject librarian, learning adviser, and learning support services librarian talk about how they collaborated to integrate AIL into the curriculum.

The assessment task for module 3 asks participants to reflect on the following:
- What is one thing you learnt from the panel discussion that made you think about collaboration in a different way?
- What actions would you like to take this year regarding collaboration?

### 7.4.4 Module 4: Integration of AIL Into the Curriculum and AIL Curriculum Design

Module 4 is designed for participants to further develop their AIL curriculum design skills by understanding and applying the Wang integration model (Wang, 2010), the RSDF (Willison & O'Regan, 2007), and Bloom's taxonomy (Bloom et al., 1956) in AIL integration and curricular development. The three key characteristics of AIL integration based on the Wang model are emphasized in the program:
- Collaboration;
- Contextualization;
- On-going interactions with information.

The assignment for module 4 requires the participants to use the courses they identified in module 2 and develop AIL learning outcomes for each of these courses (one course for each year) by applying Bloom's and RSDF. They also need to choose an existing assignment from one of these identified courses and modify it by integrating AIL with explanations of why and how they have modified it.

### 7.4.5 Module 5: Measuring the Impact of AIL Integration

Module 5 is a self-paced online learning module. Feedback from the 2015 cohort indicated that the module was too long, so we are currently revising the module to reduce content and focus on the evaluation and impact of AIL integration.

The module covers how to use evidence to measure the impact of AIL integration; the program, departmental, and course curriculum review process at the University; and self-reflection on AIL integration.

The assignment for module 5 requires participants to complete a series of activities based on readings. Below are some example activities.
1. Search the literature and find a diagnostic assessment tool that can be used in AIL integration. In your assignment sheet record the details of the article/chapter, and briefly explain the nature of the diagnostic assessment tool and why you think it might be a useful way to support student learning.
2. The University course evaluation question bank will be reviewed shortly. The current bank does not include any suitable AIL-related questions. One area where Libraries and Learning Service might contribute at a university level would be to propose a series of questions related to AIL integration. Please list 3—5 questions that you would like to use to evaluate the impact of our AIL integrations as part of the UoA course evaluation question bank.
3. Read this article: *explain* the main differences between evidence-based evaluation and perception-based evaluation. *Reflect* on the evidence that you would need to gather to demonstrate that students have learned intended AIL capabilities for a particular academic course that you are involved with. *Record* two questions that you would ask to gather this evidence and reflect on how the answers to each of these will measure the impact of our work.

Twenty-five LLS staff (including subject librarians and learning advisers) completed the program in 2012, 2013, and 2015. Feedback from the 2015 cohort, who completed the revised program, was very positive. Many commented that the program provided them with a good foundation of curriculum mapping and design as well as curriculum-related University policies and guidelines. One participant commented, "I really had a shift in thinking through participating in this program. I now think like an academic rather than just a librarian." They also made some valuable suggestions for the program. Based on feedback from participants and facilitators, the program is being revised and will be offered again in 2016.

## 7.5 CONCLUSION

The benefits of both these staff development programs are apparent. For example, student-centered teaching pedagogy has become the norm within LLS and the quality of staff members' teaching skills has improved. More AIL integration projects have been initiated by subject librarians and learning advisers at the University. More subject librarians, learning advisers, and learning support services librarians are working collaboratively with faculty teaching staff on AIL integration to scaffold and support students. Subject librarians and learning advisers have become more involved in faculty or departmental curriculum review projects and curriculum planning meetings.

Both programs will continue to be dynamic and responsive to feedback from participants to ensure they meet the evolving role of librarians in the academic environment.

## REFERENCES

Bell, S., Dempsey, L., & Fister, B. (2015). *New roles for the road ahead: Essays commissioned for ACRL's 75th anniversary.* Chicago, IL: The Association of College & Research Libraries, a division of the American Library Association.

Bloom, B. S., Engelhart, M. D., Furst, E. J., Hill, W. H., & Krathwohl, D. R. (1956). *Taxonomy of educational objectives: The classification of educational goals: Handbook 1, Cognitive domain* (Vol. 1). New York: David McKey Company, Inc.

The Charles A. Dana Center. (n.d.). Learning and the adolescent mind: Culture of learning. Retrieved from: http://learningandtheadolescentmind.org/ideas_community.html.

Delaney, G., & Bates, J. (2015). Envisioning the academic library: A reflection on roles, relevancy and relationships. *New Review of Academic Librarianship, 21*(1), 30−51. Available from http://dx.doi.org/10.1080/13614533.2014.911194.

Gillingham, E. (2013). Re-conceptualizing the role of librarians. In: Societies libraries. Retrieved from: http://exchanges.wiley.com/blog/2013/10/17/re-conceptualizing-the-role-of-librarians/.

Jaguszewski, J. M., & Williams, K. (2013). *New roles for new times: Transforming liaison roles in research libraries.* Washington, DC: Association of Research Libraries. Retrieved from: http://www.arl.org/storage/documents/publications/nrnt-liaison-roles-revised.pdf.

Johnson, K. E. (2009). *Second language teacher education: A sociocultural perspective.* New York, London: Routledge.

Lippincott, J. K. (2015). The future for teaching and learning: Librarians' deepening involvement in pedagogy and curriculum. Retrieved from: http://americanlibrariesmagazine.org/2015/02/26/the-future-for-teaching-and-learning/.

Moselen, C., & Wang, L. (2014). Integrating information literacy into academic curricula: A professional development program for librarians at the University of Auckland. *Journal of Academic Librarianship, 40*(2), 116−123. Available from http://dx.doi.org/10.1016/j.acalib.2014.02.002.

QS. (2016). QS World University Rankings 2015/16. Top Universities, Worldwide university ranking, guide & events. Retrieved from: http://www.topuniversities.com/university-rankings/world-university-rankings/2015#sorting=rank+region=+country=+faculty=+stars=false+search=.

Vygotsky, L. S. (1978). *Mind in society: The development of higher psychological processes.* Cambridge: Harvard University Press.

Vygotsky, L. S. (1981). The instrumental method in psychology. In J. Wertsch (Ed.), *The concept of activity in Soviet psychology* (pp. 3−35). Armonk, NY: Sharpe.

Wang, L. (2010). *Integrating information literacy into higher education curricula: An IL curricular integration model*. PhD thesis. Australia: Queensland University of Technology. Retrieved from: http://eprints.qut.edu.au/41747/.

Wang, L. (2013). An IL integration model and its application in curriculum integration and staff development in higher education. In: Paper presented at the European conference on information literacy, Istanbul. Retrieved from: http://link.springer.com/book/10.1007/978-3-319-03919-0.

Wang, L., Bruce, C. S., & Hughes, H. E. (2011). Sociocultural theories and their application in information literacy research and education. *Australian Academic & Research Libraries*, 42(4), 296–308.

Willison, J., & O'Regan, K. (2007). Commonly known, commonly not known, totally unknown: A framework for students becoming researchers. *Higher Education Research & Development*, 26(4), 393–409. <http://www.tandfonline.com/doi/abs/10.1080/07294360701658609#.VOOxq-aUfzg>.

CHAPTER 8

# IMPACT Lessons: Strategically Embedding Media and Information Literacy Through Teacher Development in Higher Education

M. Flierl, C. Maybee, C.F. Riehle and N. Johnson
Purdue University, West Lafayette, IN, United States

## 8.1 INTRODUCTION

Conversations about learning can, and should, involve discussions of media and information literacy (MIL). Embedding MIL meaningfully and thoughtfully into curricula is a powerful way to create richer learning experiences for students. Our approach to this work elevates academic librarians from service providers to collaborators, shifting libraries from merely providing space for learning towards becoming the place of learning. MIL-related discussions are necessary to have as teaching and learning environments change, for example, incorporating more active learning. As students are asked to do more in class, they will inevitably interact with information in more complex ways.

In helping address the needs of higher education learners, academic librarians must be able to determine the best ways to teach students to use information. While librarians working outside of the library is not as common as it should be, this chapter investigates how librarians can partner with others on campus to advance MIL. Specifically, we will describe how librarians can help integrate MIL activities into foundational courses through discussions about student learning. To address this we draw from educational and library and information science theories, as well as our experiences working with the IMPACT (Instruction Matters: Purdue Academic Course Transformation) program, a teacher development initiative at Purdue University.

We describe how the IMPACT program, which focuses on the development of student-centered teaching and learning, provides opportunities for librarians to engage with teachers about MIL. The dialogue generated by the program about student-centered teaching and learning is crucial. This is where Purdue librarians have found common ground on which to have productive MIL conversations. Conversations about learning outcomes, assessments, and classroom activities provide opportunities to embed MIL meaningfully in the context of the course.

In IMPACT, the role of the librarian shifts from liaison to consultant. Taking on this new role addresses numerous challenges including differences in institutional teaching and learning cultures, aligning MIL goals with programmatic goals, and navigating a variety of perspectives on instruction, student learning, and student information use.

Throughout this chapter, we describe how working with teachers to enhance student learning provides opportunities for integrating MIL meaningfully into foundational courses. The first three sections discuss librarian involvement in IMPACT, the shifting role of liaisons to information consultants, and how librarians utilize principles of instructional design, all to embed MIL into foundational courses. The final section offers two reflections from IMPACT librarians working with a communication and a technology course. Each reflection displays how information consulting, informed learning, and instructional design coalesce to yield more complex engagements with information while also augmenting student learning. Throughout the chapter we distill pragmatic principles from our experiences in IMPACT that can be applied across a wide variety of educational contexts and institutions.

## 8.2 TEACHER DEVELOPMENT INITIATIVES: A MIL OPPORTUNITY

In 2011, Purdue Libraries partnered with several other units on campus, including the Center for Instructional Excellence (CIE) and Information Technology at Purdue (ITaP), to create the IMPACT program. Funded by the Provost, the IMPACT program strives to create student-centered teaching and learning environments for large, undergraduate classes by empowering teachers to develop innovative educational practices. Purdue librarians serve on teams that guide teachers through the 13-week program.

An ambitious effort, IMPACT works with approximately 50 teachers per year. IMPACT is part of a set of strategic University-wide priorities labeled as "Purdue Moves." One priority is transformative education, which has the goal to give students greater access to effective approaches to teaching and learning. Teachers are incentivized to participate in

IMPACT through grants that can be used to enhance the course. A key element of the program is that the teachers have ownership of the redesign process, making changes to the course intended to address learning challenges they witness students having in their courses. Thus, there is no pressure to flip or put course content online. Each redesign is completely tailored to teacher needs.

Rather than focusing on what they, as teachers, want to "cover" in terms of course content, IMPACT encourages teachers to focus on what students will "uncover" (Crouch & Mazur, 2001; Mazur, 1997). The shift in perspective is subtle but important. The focus of instruction shifts away from the teacher towards the student (Barr & Tagg, 1995; Johnson & Swan, 1961). To facilitate the development of new approaches to learning, teachers in the program go through a backward design process involving three steps: (1) identify desired learning; (2) determine acceptable evidence of learning; and (3) plan learning experiences in instruction (Wiggins & McTighe, 2005). This design process keeps student learning at the forefront of instructional design. Hence, IMPACT's goal of a student-centered learning environment.

IMPACT Librarians work in teams of six across the 13-week semester. Each team is comprised of six people—three teachers, one instructional developer, one educational technologist, and one librarian. While many redesign programs tend to be confined to one department, IMPACT is unique in terms of the interdisciplinarity of the teachers that participate, hailing from 10 of the 11 colleges of Purdue. To support the needs of each course while integrating MIL into coursework, Purdue librarians have adopted a type of "information consultant" model for working in IMPACT.

In working with teachers from various academic disciplines, IMPACT librarians must navigate a variety of perspectives that teachers may hold about teaching and learning, and about MIL. One of the key ideas that underpins Purdue Libraries approach to MIL is derived from studies into teachers' and students' experiences of information literacy. This research shows that students typically use information with more complexity and versatility when focused on learning about a topic, rather than simply learning about information skills on their own (e.g., Lupton, 2008; Maybee, 2006). Learners' abilities to search for information have also been shown to be related to how comprehensively they can understand the topic they are studying (Limberg, 1999). However, educators sometimes view MIL as a set of discrete skills that are not directly relatable to disciplinary learning outcomes (Webber, Boon, & Johnston, 2005). MIL may be thought of as something extra, that should be taught by someone else (Webber & Johnston, 2005), or, at least, that there is no room for it in a disciplinary course (Feind, 2008). This is where informed learning (Bruce, 2008) comes to the fore.

Grounded in learning theory (Marton & Tsui, 2004), informed learning suggests that using information may be considered the "process" of learning about subject content (Lupton, 2008). For example, "collecting and analyzing" texts by select authors may be considered the process by which a learner comes to understand the Bloomsbury literary movement. Informed learning posits that using information may lead to learning, but also suggests that the two may occur simultaneously (Bruce, 2008). Thus, informed learning offers a model for embedding MIL while addressing a teacher's goals for student learning. Designing instructional activities for informed learning involves identifying subject-focused learning outcomes, and then being intentional about how the students will use information to meet those outcomes. Informed learning offers three key principles that are necessary for enabling the integration of MIL into a disciplinary learning context:

- Build on learners' existing experiences of using information to learn;
- Learning designs focus simultaneously on MIL and disciplinary learning outcomes; and
- Students become aware of new ways of using information and understanding disciplinary content (Hughes & Bruce, 2012).

This conceptual understanding of the relationship between learning and using information can be difficult to convey to teachers more accustomed to a procedural, skills-based approach to MIL. Goals such as finding and evaluating information can be easy enough to communicate. Engaging in dialogue with teachers about students using information creatively and reflectively to learn subject content is more difficult. Informed learning also places an emphasis on disciplinary uses of information (Bruce, 2008). Operationally, this involves librarians and other IMPACT team members discussing how information is used in class within the teacher's disciplinary language. For example, instead of espousing the virtues of students using information in more discrete, specific ways, IMPACT team members might suggest that students use publicly available data-sharing repositories to find datasets (instead of being given data). Grounded in an information consultant model (Frank & Howell, 2003; Frank, Raschke, Wood, & Yang, 2001; Vickers, 1992), IMPACT librarians take a strategic approach to working with teachers to consider MIL and other innovative educational ideas.

## 8.3 LIBRARIANS AS INFORMATION CONSULTANTS

The consulting approach used by the librarians came about as a result of working in IMPACT and was aligned with already-existing information consulting models (Frank & Howell, 2003; Frank et al., 2001; Vickers, 1992). The key characteristics of information consulting models relevant for academic librarians are:
- Knowledge/abilities;
- Relationship building; and
- Developing and accomplishing goals (adapted from Frank & Howell, 2003; Frank, et al., 2001; Vickers, 1992).

The knowledge/abilities needed by a consultant include being able to work in teams and within institutional constructs. Relationship building involves being able to integrate into a scholarly community and engage with scholars as equal partners. Finally, developing and accomplishing goals includes sharing solutions around a client's, namely a teacher's, actual needs and promoting a variety of solutions, some of which will certainly fail. These are different from traditional liaison skills and highlight the shifting roles of librarians as they engage with MIL and student learning in collaboration with partners outside of the library.

The information consultant model adopted by librarians working in IMPACT helps them work strategically to empower teachers to enable informed learning in their classrooms. One challenge is the difference in teaching and learning cultures across colleges at Purdue. Each college and department has its own views about how students learn within their discipline.

There is a subtle difference between cooperation and collaboration. Consulting is not concerned with cooperation, "where either party has its own goals and both cooperate for the purpose of achieving those goals" (Frank et al., 2001). A basic one-shot instruction session is a perfect example. A teacher asks a librarian to give a basic lecture on library resources or searching strategies so that students are better prepared for an upcoming assignment. The librarian furthers MIL efforts while the teacher believes she is preparing her students for success. While the two goals may be complementary, the MIL instruction is not designed to meet the specific learning goals of the assignment. Both parties further *their own goals*.

Consulting is concerned with collaboration, which involves all parties bringing their goals to the partnership, but also involves defining and working together toward *shared* goals. If the teacher and librarian of the previous example were able to meaningfully discuss the learning goals of the assignment, they could collaborate to facilitate student learning together. Perhaps the students are better served by materials the librarian did not plan to use, or the teacher was unaware of valuable information resources outside of the library. It is in this spirit that the CIE, ITaP, Libraries, and other units at Purdue work together on IMPACT. Each has its own goals, such as the Libraries' goal of more creative and reflective engagements with information to learn disciplinary content. Each team member from the three units then acts as a consultant, each with a particular expertise. However, all parties have agreed to work toward empowering teachers to foster student-centered teaching and learning environments.

Pragmatically, librarians working in IMPACT have found it ineffectual for MIL to be at the forefront of the discussion. MIL, without context, can be difficult to translate and communicate. Adopting an informed learning approach, librarians have found greater success in embedding MIL and marketing the library as a place of learning if conversations revolve around student learning, that is, learning outcomes, assessments, and classroom activities. It is around these topics where productive MIL conversations take place. This strategy anchors MIL to what teachers already find important, circumventing technical discussions about MIL that teachers rarely find of interest. Demonstrating how a reflective interaction with information will yield greater student learning, or make for a more engaging classroom activity, is of interest for teachers. In IMPACT, we have found success in building a common conversation between librarians and teachers by starting dialogue in the disciplinary language of the teacher and focusing on particular aspects of student learning. Once this common ground is reached, a librarian can have more meaningful dialogue about how students use information to learn, a conversation that continues throughout the design process.

## 8.4 OPPORTUNITIES FOR MIL THROUGH INSTRUCTIONAL DESIGN

The first weeks of IMPACT are dedicated towards teachers deciding on what they want their students to know, do, and value through rewriting course learning goals. In reflecting on their course, teachers typically shift their expectations for learning from lower-order thinking skills such as memorization, to affective and higher-order thinking skills like analyzing or evaluating (Anderson & Krathwohl, 2001; Krathwohl, Bloom, & Masia, 1956). This presents goals each IMPACT team can work towards. At times, this includes intense discussions about MIL, but sometimes those conversations do not occur until later in the process. Identifying clear and measurable learning goals for a class allows each support team to know exactly what each teacher wants to accomplish. IMPACT librarians and other team members find common goals and common ground on which to communicate and work, obviating cultural barriers to productive dialogue. This serves as an integral first step in the collaboration.

It can be challenging to align MIL goals with IMPACT goals. How does MIL help create a student-centered teaching and learning environment for an aviation technology course? At what point in the design process is it appropriate to discuss MIL when working with an anthropology professor? This challenge may be exacerbated by the inherent complexity of redesigning a course. How students interact with information can *appear* trivial to a teacher struggling with how to motivate students to read before class or find ways for them to think critically. Embracing the role of a consultant as opposed to a service provider is helpful for these issues. Listening more than one speaks, for example, is valuable not only for learning about the particular issues a teacher wants to solve, but also for building rapport with a teacher. Listening more about their concerns, their previous efforts, helps bring the IMPACT team into the instructors' scholarly community.

If instructors believe that the members of their IMPACT team understand their particular pedagogical issues, then they will be far more likely to listen to a suggestion, including suggestions about MIL. Determining student learning goals, for example, often leads to conversations about students using information. Given that a teacher wants students to learn to analyze X, or solve Y, a librarian can ask how students use information to analyze or solve. This does not need to be prescriptive or a marketing of library interests. Rather, teachers coming to reflect on *how* information is being used by students in order to learn is deemed a success within IMPACT. In fact, teachers may understand the information required for student learning better than the librarian. The Purdue Libraries' approach to MIL, informed learning, is telling here. The informed learning approach to MIL emphasizes learning as an outcome of engaging with information. If students use information to learn, then using information in more creative and reflective ways may yield greater learning (Bruce, 2008).

Teachers exploring assessment and active learning techniques can also provide opportunities to discuss MIL. Teachers must consider students' capabilities coming into the course, and determine what students still need to learn to do in order to successfully complete course assessments. In an active learning classroom, assessments, such as projects, posters, reports, and so forth, often require the students to use information in ways that are new to them. Therefore, MIL frequently comes to the fore when team members are working with a teacher to identify the learning activities that students will engage in to foster the learning outcomes the teacher envisions. In working with teachers to determine learning activities, one strategy is to offer a variety of possibilities. If all suggestions revolve around the learning outcomes then they are more likely to find an interested audience. Flatly suggesting an MIL-related activity for students to perform in a class may fall on deaf ears. A more productive approach might involve suggesting a MIL-related activity that ties directly to a learning goal, such as reflecting on what counts as authoritative information for the purpose of a specific assignment.

Active learning activities frequently result in more interactions with information outside of the teacher's watchful eye. This provides an opportunity for a librarian to ask—*how* do you, as a teacher, want students to engage with information relevant to the discipline? For example, rather than assigning readings, a librarian may encourage a teacher to task the students with finding their own examples of specific subject content to bring to class. In addition to including the extra step of finding reputable information, which may organically introduce ideas such as how information has value, the students will be interacting with information that they find interesting and relevant.

Mapping MIL suggestions to what teachers want to accomplish is key, and a librarian needs to invest time listening to what each teacher wants their students to know, do, or value. In problem-based learning, for example, students are tasked to address an open-ended question. Part of the problem-solving process is identifying what information will be needed to present a viable solution. This is an excellent opportunity to embed MIL. Students could utilize various types of media, such as a social media platform like Twitter, pulling information from one of Twitter's APIs to collect real-time data. A simpler example could involve ad hoc working groups in class. Why not utilize the wealth of information available to students given the ubiquity of cellphones and laptops? Rather than give students a newspaper article to work from, tasking students to find a reputable — newspaper or magazine article, during class, might lead to discussions about how (or if) authority is constructed. Building student MIL competence is a necessary consideration wherever students are required to intentionally engage with information. The following reflections by IMPACT librarians exemplify how consulting with teachers to design learning experiences may foster informed learning.

## 8.5 EMBEDDING MIL THROUGH CONSULTATION: IMPACT LIBRARIAN REFLECTIONS

### 8.5.1 IMPACT Librarian Reflection 1: Communication Course

Since 2011, I've served as a consultant for over 15 IMPACT course redesigns. One of the most fruitful collaborations has been with a teacher in Communication, one of my liaison areas. The course is COM 217: Science Communication, a core course required of all undergraduate students in Purdue's College of Science, and designed to build students' capacity to effectively communicate scientific and technical information to a variety of audiences.

#### 8.5.1.1 Informed Learning in the Communication Course

Informed learning is intrinsic in a course designed to build science students' capacity to communicate information. Being able to access, evaluate, and use a variety of information sources is essential for success. The course design values and utilizes knowledge and practices with which students tend to be familiar (e.g., Google searching, Wikipedia, science news, blogs, and podcasts) and builds upon those when delving into others (Google Scholar, strategic searching, and research databases) in later assignments. This allows for discussion and exploration of the differences between and among various sources and information practices. While students are using information in the course to prepare for and integrate into presentations and other assignments, they are exploring important and complicated concepts, or frames as per the ACRL Framework for Information Literacy in Higher Education (Association of College and Research Libraries, 2015) related to science information and communication: for instance, scholarship is a conversation; research is an iterative process; authority is constructed and contextual; and information has value. Understanding these concepts is key for any information-savvy individual, but in the context of science communication especially relevant for future scientists who will actively participate in discovery and communicating

**Table 8.1** Examples of informed learning in the communication course

| Principles | Examples |
|---|---|
| Builds on students' existing knowledge | Values and acknowledges students' current practices finding, evaluating, and communicating about science-related information (Google searching, Wikipedia, science news, blogs, and podcasts) and build upon these when requiring others (Google Scholar, strategic searching, and research databases) for later assignments |
| Learning focuses simultaneously on both using information and subject content | Requires the use and interpretation of a variety of scientific information sources for presentations and other assignments<br>Embeds key concepts/frames relevant to scientists' information and communication practice, via discussion and reflection, while students engage with, integrate, and create information in presentations and other assignments |
| Students become aware of new ways of using information and understanding subject content | Students should be able to consider and interpret context (audience, purpose, author's expertise/experience/perspective) as they use and create science-related information sources<br>Students should be able to critically evaluate science information sources beyond the application of standard evaluative criteria, considering methodology, communication strategies, and context |

research for years to come. A key goal of the course is that students can select and communicate information for a particular audience. Making information decisions that consider the importance of *context* (as it relates to both evaluating and communicating information) is critical. This is a challenging concept and skill for students to grasp, but one that will surely serve them well in current and future academic and professional spheres (Table 8.1).

### *8.5.1.2 Information Consulting in the Communication Course*

Before IMPACT, I did not have a professional relationship with this disciplinary colleague. Demonstrating a willingness to listen and learn about her course-related goals and challenges was essential for building trust and rapport. When consulting, I strive to employ active listening to demonstrate engagement, and I often paraphrase what I think I'm hearing and ask clarification questions to ensure I understand. Because of my own communication style, I often reflect after (mostly) listening, then follow-up

**Table 8.2** Elements of consultation in the communication course

| Characteristics | Examples |
|---|---|
| Knowledge/abilities | Employed active listening to reflect engagement and to clarify goals and perspectives<br>Motivated by and shared experience with and engagement in scholarly communities related to instructional design, active learning pedagogy, and media and information literacy (MIL) instructional theory |
| Relationship building | Followed up on meetings by sharing tailored ideas and resources to address goals and challenges discussed<br>Shared personal and theoretical approaches to MIL instruction |
| Developing and accomplishing goals | Regularly inquired about and clarified instructor and course goals<br>Suggested a variety of tailored potential strategies, including activities, assignments, and assessments |

in-person or via email with relevant and customized ideas and resources, some of which we pursue further or implement as part of the iterative redesign process. IMPACT provided me an opportunity to share, in the context of the course, my perspective on and approach to MIL and teaching and learning. I shared, for example, how and why my approach to MIL had shifted through the years from primarily emphasizing skills to engaging students in work related to higher-order, transferable concepts. As the instructor began to articulate her own approach and goals related to MIL, I even shared (as they were released) drafts of the ACRL *Framework for Information Literacy in Higher Education* (Association of College and Research Libraries, 2015), which led to a few rich conversations. I think these conversations increased my credibility and enabled me to be perceived as a member of my colleague's scholarly community, and as a collaborator in teaching and research. This even resulted in a collaborative research project related to the integration of MIL in the course soon after the instructor completed the IMPACT redesign process (Table 8.2).

## 8.5.2 IMPACT Librarian Reflection 2: Technology Course

TECH 120: Design Thinking in the Purdue Polytechnic Institute is a first-year introductory course to the design process. This course is required within the Purdue Polytechnic Institute for many of its 36 undergraduate degrees. Within the course, students learn the five main steps of the design thinking process of problem solving in technology and engineering: (1) define the problem, (2) draft a problem statement, (3) ideation, (4) evaluation, and (5) communication. Within each of these steps are opportunities for informed learning for the students, and consulting regarding infusing information literacy practices and content into the course with the instructor. In this course, I played a progressively developing role: as an instructional designer, as an embedded librarian, and most recently, an instructor of one of the sections. Although I was not a part of the original redesign 5 years ago, I have played one or all of these roles in the two and a half years I've been involved with this course.

#### 8.5.2.1 Informed Learning in the Technology Course

In TECH 120, MIL is drawn together with content-focused learning. Near the beginning of the course, students watch an instructional video about keyword selection and specific database searching. Then, they have an assignment that asks them to document finding and selecting sources in those databases. In any subsequent assignments related to the content of the course, the students are asked for annotated bibliographies and citations related to the existing coursework. As an example, there is a benchmarking assignment where students are asked to find existing solutions for a problem. These solutions can be industrial solutions or research from labs and universities. As a part of this assignment, students are asked to document their search strategy and cite those existing solutions. The new solutions that the students create are directly shaped by the information that was found and documented with their research. Similar opportunities to demonstrate their informed learning are integrated at each step of the design process, and again as a part of the final design project. Each related rubric contains elements of the informed learning strategy, techniques, and/or skills expected to be demonstrated in that assignment (Table 8.3).

#### 8.5.2.2 Information Consulting in the Technology Course

A distinguishing characteristic of this course is the ability of the embedded librarian to participate as an equal partner in the instructional process. The instructional team of the course consists of instructors, course graders, and graduate students. I have been a part of the weekly instructional team meetings, contributing to the detailed conversations about the course and the assignments, as any other member of the team. These interactions have strengthened the relationships of the library and course

Table 8.3 Examples of informed learning in the technology course

| Principles | Examples |
| --- | --- |
| Builds on students' existing knowledge | Media and information literacy (MIL) instructional videos are assigned for homework, which provide the foundation for future MIL assignments |
| Learning focuses simultaneously on both using information and subject content | As a part of defining the problem and ideating new solutions, students are required to research background information about the problem and existing solutions, which are existing course activities |
| Students become aware of new ways of using information and understanding subject content | Library-related assignments and accountability for new information in subsequent assignments, including bibliographies, quizzes, and integration into final project |

Table 8.4 Elements of consultation in the technology course

| Characteristics | Examples |
| --- | --- |
| Knowledge/abilities | Actively listen to the intentions of the faculty<br>Customize information content to fit the existing course content<br>Engage scholars as equal partners by recognizing and discussing the research opportunities from the course transformations |
| Relationship building | Attend weekly course-level instructional team meetings<br>Actively contribute to conversations about lesson planning and activities |
| Developing and accomplishing goals | Identify goals of course iterations<br>Revise existing strategies and identify new strategies for meeting instructional goals with each iteration |

coordinators, while also providing opportunities for refined iterations of the MIL instructional content over time and practice. Joint and single-authored original research has resulted from the relationship. Similarly, the course content has been refined almost every semester, occasionally in real-time, because of the entire team's investment in the success of the course and the students (Table 8.4).

## 8.6 CONCLUSION

In this chapter, we have described how librarians at Purdue leverage opportunities afforded by the IMPACT program to empower higher education teachers to strategically embed MIL into course curricula. Many development programs at other campuses may not operate on the same scale as IMPACT. Nevertheless, groups or units on other campuses investing in the development of innovative approaches to teaching and learning may provide collaborative opportunities for working with teachers to embed MIL in meaningful ways. Informed learning, with its emphasis on learning as a result of using information in intentional ways, may serve as an approach to embed MIL that resonates with teachers. The information consulting approach described in this chapter emphasizes strategies that help develop shared goals across disciplinary boundaries. As such, it is a flexible approach to collaboration with disciplinary teachers. Consulting enables teachers to see the value of MIL on their own terms, providing a pathway for working together to design MIL activities that meet the learning needs of students in higher education. We also discussed the core components of backwards design, namely learning goals, assessment, and classroom activities, and how it may provide specific targets for conversations about how students can use information more creatively and reflectively to learn subject content. Lastly, the two reflections display how the collaborations born from IMPACT require various skills and lead to different, yet successful, outcomes.

MIL and student learning are intertwined. IMPACT librarians have found that focusing on student learning is an effective way to collaborate, as opposed to cooperate, with teachers. Learning is the common thread that ties MIL together with teaching and learning initiatives, information consulting, and instructional design.

## REFERENCES

Anderson, L. W., & Krathwohl, D. R. (Eds.), (2001). *A taxonomy for learning, teaching, and assessing: A revision of Bloom's Taxonomy of Educational Objectives* New York: Longman.

Association of College and Research Libraries. (2015). *Framework for information literacy for higher education*. Association of College and Research Libraries. Retrieved from: http://www.ala.org/acrl/standards/ilframework.

Barr, R. B., & Tagg, J. (1995). From teaching to learning: A new paradigm for undergraduate education. *Change, 27*(6), 12–25.

Bruce, C. S. (2008). *Informed learning*. Chicago, IL: American Library Association.

Crouch, C. H., & Mazur, E. (2001). Peer instruction: Ten years of experience and results. *American Journal of Physics, 69*(9), 970–977.

Feind, R. (2008). Results of a phenomenographic investigation of how faculty and staff perceive, engage in, and view information literacy. *The International Journal of Learning*, *14*(12), 167−170.

Frank, D., & Howell, E. (2003). New relationships in academe: Opportunities for vitality and relevance. *College and Research Libraries News*, *64*(1), 24−27.

Frank, D., Raschke, G., Wood, J., & Yang, J. (2001). Information consulting: The key to success in academic libraries. *Journal of Academic Librarianship*, *27*(1), 90−96.

Hughes, H., & Bruce, C. S. (2012). Snapshots of informed learning: LIS and beyond. *Education for Information*, *29*, 253−269.

Johnson, V., & Swan, B. (1961). Cult of content. *Educational Leadership*, *19*(2), 118−121.

Krathwohl, D. R., Bloom, B. S., & Masia, B. B. (1956). *Taxonomy of educational objectives: The classification of educational goals. Handbook II, the affective domain*. New York: David McKay Company.

Limberg, L. (1999). Experiencing information seeking and learning: A study of the interaction between two phenomena. *Information Research*, *5*(1). Retrieved from http://informationr.net/ir/5-1/paper68.html.

Lupton, M. (2008). *Information literacy and learning*. Blackwood, Australia: Auslib Press.

Marton, F., & Tsui, A. (2004). *Classroom discourse and the space of learning*. Mahwah, NJ: L. Erlbaum Associates.

Maybee, C. (2006). Undergraduate perceptions of information use: The basis for creating user-centered student information literacy instruction. *Journal of Academic Librarianship*, *32*(1), 79−85.

Mazur, E. (1997). *Peer instruction: A user's manual*. Upper Saddle River, NJ: Prentice Hall.

Vickers, P. (1992). Information consultancy in the UK. *Journal of Information Science*, *18*, 259−267.

Webber, S., Boon, S., & Johnston, B. (2005). A comparison of UK academics' conceptions of information literacy in two disciplines: English and marketing. *Library and Information Research*, *29*(93), 4−15.

Webber, S., & Johnston, B. (2005). Information literacy in the curriculum: Selected findings from a phenomenographic study of UK conceptions of, and pedagogy for, information literacy. In C. Rust (Ed.), *Improving student learning: Diversity and inclusivity: Proceedings of the 11th ISL Symposium* (pp. 212−224). Birmingham: Oxford Brookes Univ.

Wiggins, G. P., & McTighe, J. (2005). *Understanding by design* (2nd ed.). Alexandria, VA: Association for Supervision and Curriculum Development.

# CHAPTER 9

# Action Research and Informed Learning for Transformative Professional Development About Information Literacy

A. Whisken
Carey Baptist Grammar School, Kew, VIC, Australia

## 9.1 INTRODUCTION

Teacher librarians have long sought ways to incorporate information literacy into the knowledge-building pedagogy and learning experiences of subject curricula. Various models describing the skills and literacies which come under the information literacy umbrella have been proposed, with digital literacies currently moving into the mix and evolving to new understandings. For the teacher librarian researcher, despite decades of practice, a clear and successful pedagogy for information literacy had seemed elusive.

The publication in 2008 of Christine Bruce's *Informed Learning* provided a new way of looking at the problem. It moves the library practitioner from a library-centric view, to seeing information literacy from the respective perspectives of discipline experts who design and teach the curriculum and of the students who experience that learning. In its focus on the zone of discipline practice, it is akin to Todd's instructional interventions (2004), to *Guided Inquiry* by Kuhlthau, Maniotes, and Caspari (2007), and to the competency-building of inquiry learning programs (Hay & Foley, 2009), but it takes a bigger step away from library practice.

Gibson-Langford (2007, 2008) looked at teacher practice and asked: what is to be learned from the way teachers build knowledge? Bruce looked at both teacher practice and student experience, asking: what learning is taking place as discipline information is accessed, managed, synthesized and new knowledge created? How can we design and teach curricula so that the use of subject content information is a learning experience in itself—so that subject content and information expertise are learned at the same time? It is a pedagogy initially designed for a tertiary situation—would it work in a secondary school? Was Informed Learning a pedagogical model that might bridge the gap between information literacy and practice in a secondary school? What would school teachers think about its applicability? What methodology would enable teachers to meaningfully explore the concept?

The author designed a research project to investigate these questions. She led 25 teachers in three case groups through a year-long project at Carey Baptist Grammar School, a secondary school in Victoria, Australia. Titled *ILARC: Informed Learning Action Research at Carey*, the project used action research as a way for case groups of teachers to learn about Informed Learning and to consider its applicability for secondary school learning. This project provides an example of how the development of information literacy pedagogies in schools can be approached in a very different way.

This chapter begins with an outline of the information literacy constructs of Informed Learning, which are the subject of the investigation, and briefly describes the research questions and methodology. The timeline and processes of the action research project are presented, followed by a brief overview of the research findings related to action research and Informed Learning. Finally, the implications for the field of information literacy education are outlined.

## 9.2 INFORMED LEARNING AND INFORMATION LITERACY

Bruce's Informed Learning brings together models developed in earlier research about information literacy education in tertiary environments (Bruce, 2008). This research explored their application within a secondary school context.

Bruce's *Seven Faces of Information Literacy* (1997) revealed different ways information use is experienced in learning. Understanding this variation enables educators to use different real life experiences as a basis for developing information use expertise. The Seven Faces are respectively: The Information Awareness and Communications Experience; The Sourcing Information Experience; The Information Process Experience; The Information Control Experience; The Knowledge Construction Experience; The Knowledge Extension Experience; and The Wisdom Experience.

In the following decade, Bruce, Edwards, and Lupton (2006) examined variation and relational learning theories to produce strategies for faculty and information professionals to develop student experiences of using information for learning. They looked at research that showed a clear relationship between ways in which university educators saw teaching and learning and their approaches to teaching graduate competencies, of which information literacy is one. The *Six Frames* conceptual model was developed to accommodate variation in ways learning and information use could be viewed, and to "encourage participants in the information literacy education arena to reflect on, and analyse, the varying implicit or explicit theoretical influences on their contexts" (Bruce et al., 2006, p. 2). The Six Frames are respectively: Content, Competency, Learning to Learn, Personal Relevance, Social Impact, and Relational.

The Informed Learning models incorporate certain understandings:
- That information is more than something to be used: that the knowing and being of an information user can be a learning experience itself (Bruce, 2008; Bruce et al., 2006; Lloyd, 2007);
- That just as people bring different views to learning, so too do they bring different views to using information for learning (Bruce, 2008; Bruce et al., 2006);
- That a variation approach and relational principles can be used by teachers to examine their practice and by students as a learning scaffold (Bruce, 2008; Bruce et al., 2006; Lupton, 2008);
- That information literacy skills embedded into curriculum discipline practice enables holistic development of those skills as a metacompetency known as Informed Learning (Bruce, 2008).

Bruce makes a distinction between information literacy and information literacy education: "Just as there is a difference between science and science education, history and history education, there is a difference between information literacy and information literacy education" (Bruce, 2008, p. 184). Information literacy education is: "enabling students to work with different ways of using information to learn; the educational framework that makes it possible for students to experience information literacy in new ways" (Bruce, 2008, p. 184).

The 21st century learning environment focus of this research project meant that ICTs (information and communication technologies) were an integral part of the investigation. Informed Learning provides well for that aspect, as it incorporates consideration of ICTs into the choices made about appropriate tools for using information to learn discipline content. An affordances view (Bower, 2008; Gill & Dalgarno, 2008) was also used to examine the ways that teachers made changes to their practices for inclusion of ICTs, although that finding is not reported in this chapter.

## 9.3 RESEARCH QUESTIONS

The overarching research question asks: How might Informed Learning concepts provide a bridge between information literacy theory and practice in a blended learning environment? Within that are more specific questions:
- Question One: how might teachers examine their practice of information literacy using the conceptual model of *Informed Learning*?
- Question Two: how might teacher practice provide students with discipline-based views and experiences of information literacy?
- Question Three: what affordances do teachers see in a learning management system to support teacher practice and student experiences of information literacy?

The main aim of the action research project was to develop a common understanding of Informed Learning to take to curriculum design so that students could experience these information literacy constructs across their learning, embedded contextually in discipline practice.

## 9.4 METHODOLOGY

Case study and action research methodologies were chosen for this qualitative study. They provided the required design structure and methods to facilitate a process of investigation of a phenomenon by several groups in an organization. Herr and Anderson (2005, p. 17) see action research as a very successful method to use in education, as it supports individual professional development as well as collaborative institutional change. Participatory action research (Kemmis & McTaggert, 2005, p. 564) was selected because it is well suited to an investigation by teachers of their own practice. The author, as both researcher and participant, facilitated the participative action research cycles of reflective practice by collaborative groups of teachers.

Use of multiple case study enabled collection of: data about the phenomenon being investigated by the action research groups (cases); contextual data about the particularities of the phenomenon manifesting in each case (Stake, 2006, pp. 30–40); and metadata about the action research process. It also gave structure for management, analysis, and interpretation of the data.

## 9.5 CONTEXT AND PARTICIPATION

The author is Head of Resource Centre at the years 7–12 campus of an inner suburban independent school in Melbourne, Australia. Middle school students explore a broad curriculum to gain exposure to many disciplines, while in the senior school students focus on a narrower range of subjects leading to the *Victorian Certificate of Education* (VCE) and the *International Baccalaureate* (IB).

The school has a lively and encouraging professional development culture that supports in-house programs as well as externally provided study. The *ILARC: Informed Learning Action Research at Carey* project invited year-long voluntary commitment from teachers to give time for four action cycles to be implemented and reported.

A general invitation was issued to teachers in three levels: year 8, year 10, and years 11 and 12 IB. The project aimed to have about seven participants in each group to allow for drop-out during the year, with the aim that each group would be sufficiently large for meaningful discussion to occur, but not so big that members would have limited opportunities for input. After a preliminary meeting to explain the project, 25 teachers opted in; only two left during its progression. Not all participants were able to attend each meeting, but there was evidence of high commitment by all throughout the project to complete the readings of each cycle, plan and carry out actions, and then report the results to the case group.

## 9.6 ACTION RESEARCH PROJECT

The project started with semistructured interviews with each participant, using questions designed to discover early perceptions about action research, information use in disciplines, and the affordances of ICT for information literacy education. There were five meetings for each case group across the year, allowing for four action research cycles. The author as participant researcher took on the role of facilitator in each case group. She provided reading materials, managed meeting calendars and reminders, recorded the meetings and took notes for follow up. An important aspect of this role was to ensure the "ambiance" of the meeting room was welcoming for people who had been teaching all day.

There were readings and discussion prompts based on chapters from *Informed Learning*. At the end of the project, semistructured exit interviews were conducted with each participant. The exit questions were designed to garner reflections about the project and action research itself; information literacy and the ideas of Informed Learning; and the affordances of the school's learning management system for information literacy learning. Data were collected by recording the interviews and meetings, as well as collecting notes submitted by participants, discussion in online spaces, and reflective memos by the researcher participant.

In the project, the author/researcher facilitated, observed, and participated in each of the three case groups undertaking their own action research cycles—Case 1: year 8; Case 2: year 10; and Case 3: years 11 and 12 IB teachers.

Data analysis using a priori and emergent grounded codes revealed reflective themes about action research for professional development as well as about the future use of Informed Learning as an information literacy pedagogy in secondary schools.

## 9.7 FINDINGS

This research answered the overarching research question, finding that *Informed Learning action research can provide a bridge between information literacy theory and practice in a secondary school blended learning environment.* In this chapter, the findings related to the research questions about action research (Question One) and Informed Learning (Question Two) are presented, including examples of key themes and participant comments. Comments are coded by participant (eg, 8.08 indicates a year 8 teacher who was the eighth member of the case group).

### 9.7.1 Finding One: Participatory Action Research Can Provide a Transformative Structure for Investigation of Informed Learning

The finding related to action research was that: *Participatory action research can provide a transformative structure for secondary teachers to investigate the Informed Learning model and reflect about action research as a professional development process.*

Each *ILARC* project case group demonstrated in varying ways that its members were enabled to undertake investigation of an identified problem using a particular model; to reflectively work through cycles of planning, action, and reflection; and to report on its application in teaching practice.

Key themes to emerge from the data analysis were *peer collegiality and cross disciplinary learning, structure,* and a *facilitator.* These are important factors in the successful use of action research professional development for Informed Learning praxis.

The data reveal a strong sense of collegiality in each *ILARC* case group. Participants were highly engaged, with enthusiastic contributions to discussion about pedagogy for information literacy and its practice and about the building of new knowledge as a result of interdisciplinary conversations. Case group members said they felt safe to express their emerging awareness of new concepts. They described a sense of "belonging to a group, sense of being welcomed and encouraged to participate and to explore ideas" (8.08) and "being with a group of people and meeting on a regular if not frequent basis and just space in which to talk about and reflect on teaching practice" (10.01).

The learning that arose from this collegiality was valued, with discussion referring to professional growth and cross-discipline perspectives. These comments are typical of teacher responses:

> I got a fantastic opportunity to share with other staff that I don't think we normally get across learning areas—looking at how we handle information in the big picture sense ... and I had insights there that I don't get any other way (8.06)
>
> [H]earing what other teachers were doing in the classroom, the challenges they were finding, talking about the different strategies, the projects that they were doing (10.03)

An aspect of this theme was that teacher and teacher librarian participants found working together brought a new dimension to their understanding of each other's roles and discipline perspectives. A teacher librarian commented about her experience of being in the year 10 interdisciplinary group, "I learnt a lot about what year 10 teachers are doing which was what I had hoped for," mentioning a particular teacher "and her amazing variety of ways and media and research activities that she does with her students" (10.04).

Through shared learning experiences, teacher librarians can become part of the teachers' views of how information is used to learn discipline content. For example, a teacher and a teacher librarian, both year 10 case group members, undertook action in the project to bring student attention to the quality and relevance of the sources they were choosing for their research. The teacher later reflected:

> I've always said in my classes you need to be able to look at sites and information you use and say what's good information and what's bad information, but then you don't do anything else about it. So I think this actually makes you stop and say, so how do you actually teach students, what is good what is bad information? How do you actually evaluate that? (10.07)

The structure of the action research project was described as a powerful professional development framework, with an IB teacher stating:

*I got lots out of this project, both in terms of what we did in the meetings, sharing ideas and gaining insights ... it made me think a lot about my own practice, and it sort of pushed me into doing a few things differently, trying to explore different ways of doing things (IB.02)*

The importance of having a facilitator to manage the project was mentioned by many, including this year 8 teacher:

*they're driven by someone who will make the meetings happen, who will make the meetings attractive to attend, and who makes sure that the planning is understood, so that I know that I need to do these things by this date ... and I know exactly what to expect along the way. (8.01)*

Some saw particular value in having a teacher librarian as facilitator, including a year 10 teacher, who said:

*it's really nice having somebody else give you the readings rather than going to the library and looking at a shelf of 20 books in an area which you want to find something that you want to explore further. And that's really valued and the support which you get through a process. (10.01)*

Teacher comments demonstrated new perceptions of the role of the teacher librarian—as an information expert who could bring particular expertise to curriculum design and delivery, and as a professional development facilitator in the organization.

### 9.7.2 Finding Two: Teachers Can "Get" Informed Learning Ideas

The finding related to Informed Learning was that: *Teachers can "get" Informed Learning ideas: the constructs of the model can enable case groups of secondary teachers to reflect about Informed Learning ideas from the context of their own views and experiences and consider their future application as an information literacy pedagogy in schools.*

Members of each *ILARC* case group demonstrated that reflective application of the ideas of Informed Learning brought about new views and practices of information literacy education. That process of gaining understanding to transfer to new discipline information literacy practices is presented as consisting of three phases: awareness, application, and transfer.

These are presented below with brief examples of teacher comments as an illustration of the way teachers can "get" Informed Learning ideas.

### 9.7.2.1 Awareness: Connecting Informed Learning Ideas to Existing Experiences

Informed Learning seeks to bring awareness that educators' experiences of information use can influence the curriculum they design and their teaching practice. This was achieved for teachers across the cases, through identification of their *existing experiences of information use* and *influences on their discipline curriculum practices and student experiences.*

#### 9.7.2.1.1 Existing Experiences of Information Use

Teacher comments related to their awareness of existing experiences of information use chiefly referred to *changes in the learning environment* and *new strategies* required by teachers and students for 21st century information use. For example, descriptions of the changes in their learning environments tended to be in terms of the challenges brought by the increased amount and range of information available. These included being "flooded with information" (8.05) and "a high level of saturation of information now compared with when we were all students" (8.06). They said that new skillsets were required: "you're accessing a whole range of information. So having that diversity of information for students to work with is probably what I see as being the key part of that Informed Learning" (8.07); and "part of this project ... is for us to get students to be better or more astute users of information" (IB.05).

Teachers articulated the need for a broader set of information strategies than the information-finding skills of the past, for example:

> creating awareness and appreciation of different ways of using information to learn, building capacity and confidence in the application of different ways of using information to learn across different contexts. It allows development of deeper and more expansive understanding, with greater ability to differentiate subtle differences ... It provides opportunity for students to access information in different ways. Makes allowance for different learning styles. (10.02)

#### 9.7.2.1.2 Influences on Discipline Curriculum Practice and Student Experiences

*Informed Learning* readings showed that curriculum can be designed to bring student attention to the Six Frames approaches of using information to learn discipline content, and to the Seven Faces experiences of combining aspects of information use. The readings also referred to the many factors that might influence teacher choices about using the constructs of each.

Teacher descriptions of possible influences on their use of the Six Frames included: *diversity of views, discipline curriculum practice*, and the relationship between their views and the *preferred frames* they use in their practice. For example, teachers in all case groups identified a diversity of views about approaches to use of information held by teachers across the disciplines as well as within a discipline, as seen in this comment:

> some teachers, they get caught on the first two of these frames and they think that's as far as I need to go, that kids need knowledge and then they need to demonstrate that they have knowledge and that's it. And then there's a whole other group of teachers within our learning area who want to push all the way through to the 6, without explicitly knowing it. It's implicit in what they do, and it can create a divergent way of thinking when it comes to curriculum development and in order to get a diverse curriculum we need to make it that we're all going through all the way to the end. (8.04)

Descriptions of influences on use of the Seven Faces included: *teacher and student information use; current discipline practices; Faces important to discipline practices and learning;* and *cross-discipline application*.

For example, when referring to influences on use of Faces important to their discipline practices, teachers often mentioned the Second Face of The Sourcing Information Experience. This can be seen in the following comment which reveals awareness of the influence of a changing relationship with source selection when teachers are no longer the intermediaries:

> we now have students talking to us about a YouTube video they found, or a song that they found interesting, that they can access. So we're no longer the main source of information, so we have to actually teach them to be discerning about what they access in relation to the topic that we're working on, and that's a new space for us. (8.06)

By using the discussion prompts of Informed Learning readings, teachers in the ILARC case groups developed awareness that their views and experiences of information use might influence their use of the Frames and Faces in design of curriculum for information literacy education.

### *9.7.2.2 Application: Reflective Application of Informed Learning Ideas to Current Practice and Experience*

Informed Learning introduced the idea that elements of the Six Frames and Seven Faces models might accord with educational directions influencing current teaching practice. This section describes how teachers in case groups applied that idea to appreciative inquiry of their own *current practices* and *student experiences*.

### 9.7.2.2.1 Current Teacher Practices

Teacher reflection about how Frames and Faces matched educational directions in their current practices produced comments about *dominant curriculum directions and discipline practices* and about *strategies significant for discipline learning*.

Where they identified Frames and Faces which accorded with dominant curriculum directions in their disciplines, it was often in combinations. For example, a teacher of LOTE (languages other than English) said that an increasing part of her professional discipline practice was keeping current (First Face) with ways to utilize the engaging information formats (Fourth Frame) available on Internet sites (Second Face) to help learning in her subject area. She said that this enabled people in her discipline area to break down previous barriers to individual progress, using these resources "at any level in the classroom ... it's something we just can't survive without now, really" (8.06).

Another example of Informed Learning strategies being identified as representing significant directions in their current discipline practice can be seen in a teacher's description of showing his students how to build competency (Second Frame) in reflective use of economics sources (Second Face). He modeled the process from year 11 by referring to economics articles in daily papers so they learned "to look at the world through economic eyes." By year 12 they were able

> to take an article and to look for two or three diagrams that will illustrate key economic issues or ideas and then to be able to evaluate that ... the students who do best are those who do think most about their work and do reflect on it. (IB.04)

For a year 8 teacher, an important curriculum direction was development of competency (Second Frame) to explore discipline themes using appropriate and unbiased online sources (Second and Third Faces), so he also modeled the expert practice he wanted them to learn:

> I present them what I've selected as a starting point, and say, "these are the reasons why I think this is a reliable source" and will go through it with them ... so they know what my parameter is and they enjoy the opportunity to go off and try and find other things on the same sort of theme. (8.03)

### 9.7.2.2.2 Current Student Experiences

Participants applied their understandings of Informed Learning to examination of how their students experienced the information practices being brought to their attention. Their comments addressed: *how those experiences were discovered*; the *different approaches to the Frames and Faces* students might experience and also bring to the experiences; and where there might be *conflicting approaches*.

Ways to discover the student experience included reflective tools, inclusion in assessment, group feedback, and individual discussion. Although there were fewer references to discovery of the student experience than those describing different approaches and possible conflicts, comments from teachers across the case groups demonstrated understanding of the diagnostic intent of the model. For example, one said that as a teacher of students for whom English was a second language, she needed to be very aware of the information practices and understandings her students brought to the learning experience, and their consequent capacities to establish veracity of information presented. "One of the things I've found that helps me in that set of problems is spending more time getting them to talk to me about their cultural values, where they've come from in terms of the belief systems they have" (IB.11).

Teachers described how students would experience a variety of the Informed Learning approaches within and across discipline areas, and also within the practices of individual teachers. For example, one teacher said she could see that she operated very much in the Learn to Learn Frame, seeing it as:

*Very valid in the case of LOTE ... the whole concept of organizing a database of vocabulary and how they structure that and how they can sort and categorize them and move them around according to each of the topic areas. (IB.06)*

This also shows her understanding that within her own practice, student attention would be brought to the Frames approaches of developing discipline competencies, and the Seven Faces idea of helping students develop a repertoire of information use strategies to apply to particular learning purposes, such as Knowledge Construction and Extension.

Reference to conflicting approaches being experienced by students—and brought by students—can be seen in a year 8 case group discussion about strategies which utilized contextual fast access to information compared with the quality that resulted. One teacher said she found that "the Internet in the classroom is totally invaluable" especially for quickly finding "snippets" of information at point of learning need (8.05). Another pointed to the engagement factor of quick graphic online information as important in maintaining attention: "Absolutely fantastic ... whereas if I'd produced a book and held a book up and said, 'Here's a pigmy possum,' then within 15 seconds the kids would have lost interest" (8.08). But others talked about the tendency for this to be the main approach, resulting in learning that was "shallow" (8.03), typifying a

> culture of finding the quick answer. Students then see that as a way of performing, finishing the task. "I'll just get this done quickly – Reptiles? Yeah okay, I can Google that." Get the quick answer, won't learn anything: Control C, Control V, on the page, bang. (8.04)

Across the case groups, teachers demonstrated that they could apply their Informed Learning understandings to examination and discussion about the different strategies currently being used to bring attention to the information approaches and experiences of the Frames and Faces. However, there were fewer references to ways that teachers discovered the student experience of those intentions, and no evidence of a consistent pattern or program which would ensure variation of experiences in the way suggested by Informed Learning—and which might overcome potentially conflicting approaches.

### 9.7.2.3 Transfer: Transfer of Informed Learning Ideas to Creation of New Discipline-Based Views and Experiences of Information Literacy

Participants showed they could transfer their understanding of Informed Learning ideas to ways of using Frames and Faces in design of new curriculum and learning activities. They referred to teaching about *discipline information sources and competencies*, encouraging *engagement and ownership of learning with information*, and to ways that they might move from a focus on *content and competency* in their disciplines to using more *learning to learn* approaches.

Most teachers implemented one or more actions in which they tried out some of these ideas with their subject classes, usually involving use of ICTs to enhance teaching and learning with information. The journal and blog tools in the school's learning management system were popular first steps. They trialed the use of these for reflections between teacher and student and for shared learning. In this way, they brought approaches of the Learning to Learn and Personal Relevance Frames in experiences which used ICT for the First Face of Information Awareness and Communication. An IB teacher said, "that was new to me all of that, so it was good just to have an intro to actually going into that medium ... it's given me a starting point" (IB.08). Others described their beginning activities: "sort of making it a conversation ... where they ask a question, and they have to provide an answer to two different people" (IB.07), and "give them specific things in Chinese, in the target language and let them ... reply" (IB.09). A year 10 teacher found it a positive step: "Good, kids like it: 'Can we put this in the journal?' ... so that's working really well" (10.05).

Others took on larger projects to try out Informed Learning ideas. For example, one teacher's action was to investigate a way to change her classroom culture to assist student discovery of expert information practices, trying to incorporate as many of the Frames and Faces as she could. It involved

> a task that took students outside specifically what they were going to get marks for in the curriculum. And for me I thought it was quite risky because I did not expect the students to want to participate ... They were scaffolded even to the extent that the first one was an artistic piece, just a drawing and a flow diagram. And the second part was a really difficult task where they had to go and access some online databases and information and create a formal scientific report, like they would do in a laboratory. And the third part was an analysis of their own carbon footprint which they did with an interactive website. And then they had to do an assessment of the significance of what they had found out and talk about the social implications.

She asked them to reflect on the experience:

> I have to say I was really pleasantly surprised because ... there was no negative feedback. ... So I thought I might try it again ... it has made me look at different ways of doing things that I had not thought would work. (10.02)

A year 8 teacher felt so confident about her actions with ICTs that she intended to incorporate Informed Learning ideas in new curriculum design for the following year: "things that I have developed solely out of what we've done in these *ILARC* sessions. ... it's given us an opportunity to introduce variety into what we're going to do next year" (8.08).

Across the case groups, teachers demonstrated that they had gained sufficient understanding about Informed Learning to undertake actions which would transfer those ideas into teaching practices and student experiences.

## 9.8 SUMMARY OF FINDINGS

Both the methodology and the subject of the research project were intentionally transformative. Three case groups of teachers at a secondary school used action research to investigate a new information literacy pedagogy and to consider its application for use in their own discipline practices. For these teachers, the combination of two deliberately transformative processes—the Informed Learning readings and discussion prompts and the action research cycles—enabled new understandings about the use of information to learn and how that might be applied in a secondary school learning environment. The processes of awareness, application, and transfer of ideas about Informed Learning bridged the gap between information literacy theory and practice for teachers, and they found action research to be a powerful professional development process.

In this research project, teacher librarians and teachers worked together through action research to explore discipline-based information literacy pedagogy and learning. There were clear structures for group formation and for learning about the use of information to learn. The project brought about changes to practice and to the ways in which teachers and teacher librarians viewed each other's roles in teaching and learning.

## 9.9 IMPLICATIONS FOR PRACTICE

This research has relevance for professional development in education using action research as well as for professional development about information literacy education. Teachers and teacher librarians in the *ILARC* project were enabled by its combination of action research and Informed Learning to move from awareness about how views and experiences of information use have an impact on curriculum design, to undertake deeper investigation and development of their practices related to the use of information to learn.

Their positive responses to action research were factors in the school's subsequent adoption of action research as a way to conduct future professional development in the school, and the style of the project has since been used in several action learning groups.

To have the teacher librarian as facilitator and to have a teacher librarian in each interdisciplinary case group was empowering, in emancipatory and transformative ways, for both teacher librarian and teacher participants. In working together, these two educator subgroups were released from the constrictions of classroom and library. The project respected and validated teachers as discipline experts and teacher librarians as information and knowledge management experts. Together they planned action research cycles to explore and develop curriculum design for variation in ways of viewing and experiencing information use in a blended learning environment. The outcome was the development of shared understandings about use of information for learning, showing that Informed Learning and action research can be used to bridge the gap between information literacy theory and practice in schools.

## REFERENCES

Bower, M. (2008). Affordance analysis — Matching learning tasks with learning technologies. *Educational Media International*, *1*(45), 3—15. Retrieved from: http://dx.doi.org/10.1080/09523980701847115.

Bruce, C. (1997). *The seven faces of information literacy*. Blackwood, Australia: Auslib Press.

Bruce, C. (2008). *Informed learning*. Chicago, IL: Association of College and Research Libraries.

Bruce, C., Edwards, S., & Lupton, M. (2006). Six frames for information literacy education. *Italics*, *5*(1). <http://www.ics.heacademy.ac.uk/italics/vol5iss1.htm>.

Gibson-Langford, L. (2007). Collaboration: Force or forced? Part 1. *Scan*, *26*(4), 19—25.

Gibson-Langford, L. (2008). Collaboration: Force or forced? Part 2. *Scan*, *27*(1), 31—37.

Gill, L., & Dalgarno, B. (2008). Influences on pre-service teachers' preparedness to use ICTs in the classroom. In: Hello! Where are you in the landscape of educational technology? Proceedings ascilite Melbourne 2008. http://www.ascilite.org.au/conferences/melbourne08/procs/gill.pdf.

Hay, L., & Foley, C. (2009). School libraries building capacity for student learning in 21C. *Scan*, *28*(2), 17—26.

Herr, K., & Anderson, G. (2005). *The action research dissertation: A guide for students and faculty*. London: Sage.

Kemmis, S., & McTaggert, R. (2005). Participatory action research: Communicative action and the public sphere. In N. Denzin, & Y. Lincoln (Eds.), *Handbook of qualitative research* (3rd ed., pp. 559—602). London: Sage.

Kuhlthau, C., Maniotes, L., & Caspari, A. (2007). *Guided inquiry: Learning in the 21st century*. London: Libraries Unlimited.

Lloyd, A. (2007). *Understanding information literacy in the workplace: Using constructivist grounded theory approach. Exploring methods in information literacy research* (pp. 67—84). Wagga Wagga, Australia: CIS.

Lupton, M. (2008). *Information literacy and learning*. Adelaide, Australia: Auslib Press.

Stake, R. (2006). *Multiple case study analysis*. New York, NY: The Guildford Press.

Todd, R. (2004). Interventions that matter: Student learning through effective school libraries. *Synergy*, *2*(1), 32—41.

# AFTERWORD

The concept of this book has evolved since 2012 when Chandos Publishing first invited Siri to submit a book proposal. At that time, Siri worked at the University of Agder with the school library studies and the Norwegian School Library Program, and Dianne was newly retired from her position in school library education at the University of Alberta. Siri invited a number of authors to join her project: Dianne and Barbara-Schultz-Jones whom she knew from work with International Federation of Library Associations (IFLA) publications and later from an information literacy conference in Oslo; Kari Flornes whom she knew from conferences in the Norwegian School Library Program; Hilde Johannessen, who was a colleague from the University of Agder and Lise A. Henrichsen, who was a colleague from several previous projects. Lise (University College UCC Regional Center for Educational Services, Copenhagen) had to step aside for various reasons, but part of her work is represented in Siri's chapter. The reviewers of the Chandos book proposal invited Siri and Dianne, as co-editors, to expand the theoretical and geographical reach of the book. We reached out to Christine Bruce, author of *Informed Learning*, and she recommended a number of authors who later came on board the project: Anne Whisken from Carey Baptist Grammar School; Li Wang and her colleague Stephanie Cook from the University of Auckland; Clarence Maybee and colleagues Michael Flierl, Catherine Fraser Riehle, and Nastasha Johnson from Purdue University; and Tina Inzerilla from Las Positas College.

In this book we have looked into different aspects of media and information literacy (MIL), and investigated how MIL can be taught in schools and universities. Our aim has been to provide university teachers and academic librarians as well as teacher education students and library students with fundamental knowledge about MIL and MIL education. Teacher education students and library students do not only need to be media and information literate themselves; they must be enabled to educate others as well.

The MIL concept has been developed over the last few decades, based on research mainly within library and information science. To some extent MIL has also been an issue in pedagogical research, however, for instance related to reading and writing education. MIL includes skills needed during the whole learning process, from acknowledging one's information needs and formulating a research question, to finding information, evaluating sources, and using the information efficiently. The concept includes the ability to communicate and share information and to evaluate one's learning outcome and learning process. In addition, using other people's creative work and research findings requires knowledge about how to cite and document the information sources. As educators we need to build awareness and attitudes that ownership and copyright are important values. Thus MIL education also involves ethical issues.

Our focus has been on process-based inquiry approaches for developing MIL, involving students in active learning and open-ended investigations and emphasizing their personal learning process. The holistic approach to create "spaces for learning" not just "places for learning" is advocated by international standards for library practice. This perspective is relevant in all teaching. It addresses the need for an educational foundation that will encourage students to incorporate innovations, draw conclusions, make informed decisions, apply knowledge to new situations, and create new knowledge. We build on sociocultural learning theory, acknowledging that students learn in a context, from each other as well as from educators, and by actively using learning resources of various kinds.

Closely connected to this understanding of teaching and learning is the concept of civic literacy, the competencies that we all need in order to participate in democratic processes. UNESCO has developed a MIL curriculum to support civic literacy programs at every level from kindergarten to higher education. This framework aims at ensuring that skills are learnt that will help the individual in a lifelong and life-wide learning process.

Several studies indicate that students need to improve their MIL, even though they are not necessarily aware of this fact themselves. Consequently, MIL must be taught in schools and universities, and in order to develop good instruction, teachers and librarians need to collaborate. It is important that a shared understanding of what MIL is and how it best can be taught is developed in schools and universities.

The Lyon Declaration on Access to Information and Development, adopted by the International Federation of Library Associations and Institutions (IFLA) in August 2014 emphasizes not only the right for all individuals to have information, but also to be provided with the competencies needed to understand and use the information. MIL education must be in place to ensure these rights.

**S. Ingvaldsen and D. Oberg**

# INDEX

*Note*: Page numbers followed by "*f*" and "*t*" refer to figures and tables, respectively.

## A

AASL. *See* American Association of School Librarians (AASL)
Academic and information literacy (AIL), 107. *See also* Media and information literacy (MIL)
   curriculum integration, 112
      into curriculum and AIL curriculum design, 115
      foundation, 114–115
      measuring impact, 115–116
   for learning, 113–114
   understanding faculty curriculum, 114
Academic integrity policies, 33
Academic librarians, 1
Academic libraries, 107
   MIL instruction in, 5
      convergences, 8–10
      framework for information literacy in higher education, 6–7
      informed learning, 7–8
Academic texts, 100
   key elements, 100–101
   peer reviewing process, 100
Accreditation organizations. *See* Community college
ACRL. *See* Association of College and Research Libraries (ACRL)
Action research
   methodologies, 138
   project, 139–140
      structure, 140, 142
Active learning activities, 126
AIL. *See* Academic and information literacy (AIL)
ALA. *See* American Library Association (ALA)
American Association of School Librarians (AASL), 14
American College and Research Libraries (ACRL). *See* Association of College and Research Libraries (ACRL)
American Library Association (ALA), 14
Anchoring, 57–60
Appreciative inquiry, 144
Association of College and Research Libraries (ACRL), 1, 14, 69, 90–91, 127–129
   ethics extracts from, 19*t*
   information literacy competency standard, 18*t*

## B

Behavioristic view of information literacy, 6, 90–91
Bloom's taxonomy, 109, 113, 115

## C

Canadian Library Association (CLA), 14
Case study methodologies, 138
Center for Instructional Excellence (CIE), 120
Centre for Learning and Research in Higher Education (CLeaR), 109
Centre for Professional Development (CPD), 109
CIE. *See* Center for Instructional Excellence (CIE)
Citation Compass, 98–99, 99*f*
Civic literacy in teacher education
   "*Educating the information-literate teacher*" project, 41–43
   media and information competences, 37–38
   MIL
      and human rights, 38–40
      religious education and, 45–47
   teacher education
      MIL approach construction, 44–45
      in Norway, 40–41

CLA. *See* Canadian Library Association (CLA)
CLeaR. *See* Centre for Learning and Research in Higher Education (CLeaR)
Collaboration, 57−60, 62−63, 67−69, 114−115, 123−124
 collaborative approach, 9−10
 by faculty, 69
 faculty's interpretation, 76
 by librarians, 69
 between library and faculty, 93
 motivating factors and challenges, 76−80
Collaborators, 70−72, 74−77, 79−82
Communication course, 127. *See also* Technology course
 elements of consultation, 129*t*
 information consulting in, 128−129
 informed learning in, 127−128, 128*t*
Community college, 68−70
Complex skills in one-shot instruction, 102
Connecting informed learning ideas to existing experiences, 143
 existing experiences of information use, 143
 influences on discipline curriculum practice and student experiences, 143−144
Consultation, embedding MIL through, 127−131
Context, 127−128, 138−139
Convergences, 8
 attending to learner's experience, 10
 collaborative approach, 9−10
 integrated approach, 9
 process approach, 9
 supporting metacognition and reflection, 10
Conversations, 119, 124−125
Cooperators, 70−72, 75−77, 79−82
CPD. *See* Centre for Professional Development (CPD)
Creativity, 78
Cross disciplinary learning, 140
Current student experiences, 145−147
Current teacher practices, 145
Curriculum Integration of Academic and Information Literacy staff development program, 109, 112
 into curriculum and AIL curriculum design, 115
 foundation, 114−115
 measuring impact, 115−116
Cyberbullying, 23−24

## D

Data analysis, 140
Design Thinking in the College of Technology, 129−130
Designing tutorials/presentations, 111
Digital library, 61
"Doing no harm" principle, 23−24

## E

"*Educating the information-literate teacher*" project, 41−43
Educational theorists, 67
"Educators of educators" concept, 2
Empathic communication, 39−40
Ethical use of information as MIL skill, 13. *See also* Teaching, ethics as MIL skill
 ethics, 13
 information literacy, 14−17
  ACRL information literacy competency standard, 18*t*
  ethics extracts from ACRL, 19*t*
  placing ethics in, 17−19
 learning environment, 24−25
Ethics, 13. *See also* Teaching, ethics as MIL skill
 extracts from ACRL framework, 19*t*
 in information literacy competences, 17−19
 integrating in teaching information literacy, 31−33
 principles for information literacy, 20
  of fair representation, 23
  of intellectual property, 21−22
  of nonmaleficence, 23−24
  of privacy, 22−23

## F

Facilitator, 140, 142
Faculty, collaboration, 69
Faculty curriculum, 114
Faculty's experience of collaboration
   faculty's interpretation
     of collaboration, 76
     of information literacy, 76
   teaching social network
     faculty's, 74–75
     influential elements in, 73–74, 73*f*
Fair representation, principle of, 23
Feedback, 9, 48–49
Five Ws approach, 96–98
   in library instruction, 98
   What, 97
   When, 97
   Where, 97
   Who, 97
   Why, 97–98
"Focus formulation stage", 95
Framework for Information Literacy in Higher Education, 91

## G

GLU 1–7 for student teachers, 41
"Google Generation", 90
Guided inquiry design framework, 27–31, 28*t*
Guided Inquiry process, 4, 4*t*

## H

Higher education, framework for information literacy in, 6–7
Human rights, MIL and, 38–40

## I

IB. *See* International Baccalaureate (IB)
ICT. *See* Information and communications technology (ICT)
IFLA. *See* International Federation of Library Associations (IFLA)
IL. *See* Information literacy (IL)
*ILARC* project. *See Informed Learning Action Research at Carey* project (*ILARC* project)
IMPACT librarian reflections
   communication course, 127–129
   technology course, 129–131
IMPACT program. *See* Instruction Matters: Purdue Academic Course Transformation program (IMPACT program)
IMRAD-structure, 101
Information and communications technology (ICT), 38
Information consultants, librarians as, 123–124
Information consulting
   in communication course, 128–129
   in technology course, 130–131
Information literacy (IL), 14, 53–54, 69–70, 89, 93–94, 107, 135
   behavioristic view, 90–91
   CLA, 14
   competence, 17
   elements of MIL, 57
   ethical principles, 20
     of fair representation, 23
     of intellectual property, 21–22
     of nonmaleficence, 23–24
     of privacy, 22–23
   faculty's interpretation, 76
   information society, 55
   informed learning and, 136–137
   key competences for lifelong learning, 15*t*
   learning center, 54
   library instruction, 89–90
   objectives of learning, 56
   phenomenographic view, 91
   placing ethics in, 17–19
   sociocultural perspective, 91–93
   teaching source criticism, 94–95
   transformation of informed learning ideas, 147–148
   Wikipedia, 55
*Information Literacy Competency Standards for Higher Education*, 6, 17
Information search process (ISP), 27
Information society, 55
Information Technology at Purdue (ITaP), 120

Informed learning, 7–8, 25, 122
  action research project, 139–140
  in communication course, 127–128, 128t
  context and participation, 138–139
  findings, 140
    connecting informed learning ideas to existing experiences, 143–144
    informed learning ideas transformation, 147–148
    participatory action research use, 140–142
    reflective application of informed learning ideas, 144–147
    teachers getting informed learning ideas, 142–148
  frames for, 26t
  implications for practice, 149–150
  and information literacy, 136–137
  methodology, 138
  research questions, 138
  in technology course, 130, 131t
*Informed Learning Action Research at Carey* project (*ILARC* project), 136, 139–140
Inquiry model, 5f
Instinctive behavior, 95
Instruction Matters: Purdue Academic Course Transformation program (IMPACT program), 119–120
  embedding MIL through consultation, 127–131
  librarians as information consultants, 123–124
  opportunities for MIL through instructional design, 124–127
  teacher development initiatives, 120–122
Instructional design
  opportunities for MIL through, 124–127
  principles, 120–121
  shared language, 54, 56–57, 84, 124
Integrated approach, 9, 56, 119–120
  principles for, 122
Intellectual property, principle of, 21–22
International Baccalaureate (IB), 138–139
International Federation of Library Associations (IFLA), 15
Internet as source for information, 101
Interviews, 71–73
ISP. *See* Information search process (ISP)
ITaP. *See* Information Technology at Purdue (ITaP)

# K

K-12 school library sector, instructional models in, 4–5
"Knowledge/abilities", 123

# L

Languages other than English (LOTE), 145
Learner's experience, attending to, 10
Learning, 92
  AIL for, 113–114
  environment, 9, 24–25
    and resources, 61
  theories, 89–93, 110–111
Librarians, 68, 89–90, 107–108
  challenges preventing collaboration with, 79–80
  collaboration by, 69
  embedded in faculty's class instruction, 80–82
  factors motivating faculty to collaborate with, 76–78
  faculty collaboration, 68–69
    information literacy, 69–70
  as information consultants, 123–124
  as instructors, 10–11, 79, 84, 90
  personal characteristics, 78
Libraries, 22–23
  students, 51
Libraries and Learning Services (LLS), 108
  staff, 112
Library and information studies (LIS), 2–3
Library faculty. *See* Librarians
Library instruction, 89–90
  five Ws approach in, 98
LIS. *See* Library and information studies (LIS)
LLS. *See* Libraries and Learning Services (LLS)
LOTE. *See* Languages other than English (LOTE)

# M

Media and information competences, 37–38
Media and information literacy (MIL), 1, 13, 37–38, 51, 93–94, 119.
  *See also* Academic and information literacy (AIL)
  academic librarians, 1
  approach construction in teacher education, 44–45
  complex set of skills, 52–53
  "educators of educators" concept, 2
  embedding MIL through consultation, 127–131
  and human rights, 38–40
  instruction in academic libraries, 5
    convergences, 8–10
    framework for information literacy in higher education, 6–7
    Informed Learning, 7–8
  instruction in school libraries, 2
    inquiry model, 5f
    instructional models in K-12 school library sector, 4–5
    K-12 students, 3–4
    seminal research, 3
  MIL-related activity for students, 126
  opportunity, 120–122
    through instructional design, 124–127
Metacognition and reflection, 10
MIL. *See* Media and information literacy (MIL)

# N

Nonacademic source evaluation, 101–102
Nonmaleficence principle, 23–24
Norway, teacher education in, 40–41
Norwegian School Library Program, 53, 60, 62

# O

One-shot instruction, 4, 9, 90, 93–94
  teaching complex skills in, 102
Organic process, 95

# P

Participants, 70–71
Participation, 138–139
Participatory action research use, 140–142
Peer collegiality, 140–141
Peer reviewing process, 100
Pestalozzi Program, 40
  of The Council of Europe, 38–39
PISA. *See* Program for International Student Assessment (PISA)
Potentials, 70–71, 73, 75–76, 79–81
Presenter Training program, 108–112
  designing tutorials/presentations, 111
  learning theories, 110–111
  teaching practices, 111
  and reflection, 111–112
Privacy, principle of, 22–23
Process approach, 2–3, 7, 9
Professional development, 138–142, 149
Program for International Student Assessment (PISA), 52
Purdue librarians, 119–121
"Purdue Moves", 120–121

# R

RE. *See* Religious education (RE)
Reflection, 3–5, 10, 27
Reflective application of informed learning ideas, 144
  current student experiences, 145–147
  current teacher practices, 145
Religious education (RE), 41, 44
  and MIL, 45–47
Research, 127–128
Research Skills Development Framework (RSDF), 113

# S

Scholarship, 127–128
School libraries
  anchoring, 57–60
  collaboration, 57–60
  information literacy, 53–57
  integrating use of libraries, 62–63
  learning environments and resources, 61

School libraries (*Continued*)
   MIL, 51−53
      inquiry model, 5*f*
      instruction, 2
      instructional models in K-12 school library sector, 4−5
      K-12 students, 3−4
      seminal research, 3
      teaching media, 53−57
*Search & Write* program, 44−46
*Seeking Meaning* text, 10
"Serious and objective" perspective, 45
Seven Faces of Information Literacy, 136, 144
Six Frames conceptual model, 136−137, 144
Social network analysis, 70−71
Sociocultural theories, 110
Source consciousness, 102−103
Source criticism
   academic texts, 100−101
   Citation Compass, 98−99, 99*f*
   delimitations, 94
   five Ws approach, 94−95
      using in library instruction, 98
   information literacy, 94−95
      and learning theories, 89−93
   Internet as source for information, 101
   MIL, 93−94
   nonacademic source evaluation, 101−102
   one-shot instruction, 93−94
      teaching complex skills in, 102
   source consciousness, 102−103
   source value identification, 101−102
   subject-specific adjustments, 93−94
   teaching students to search for and assess sources, 95−96
Source value identification, 101−102
Staff development programs
   curriculum integration of AIL program, 112−116
   Presenter Training program, 109−112
   University of Auckland LLS, 108−109
*Standards for the 21st Century Learner*, 14, 17
Student role in MIL, 40, 60
Student-centered learning activities, 112, 126
Subject-specific adjustments, 93−94

## T

*Tasks for Democracy*, 38−39
Teacher development initiatives, 120−122
Teacher education
   MIL approach construction, 44−45
   in Norway, 40−41
   students, 51
Teacher librarians, 135, 141−142, 149−150
Teachers getting informed learning ideas, 142−148
Teaching
   ethics as MIL skill, 25
   frames for informed learning, 26*t*, 31
   guided inquiry design framework, 27−31, 28*t*
   use of scenarios, 27
   media, 53−54
      elements of MIL, 57
      information society, 55
      learning center, 54
      objectives of learning, 56
      Wikipedia, 55
   practices, 111
   and reflection, 111−112
Teaching faculty collaboration with academic librarians, 67−68
   challenges preventing collaboration with librarians, 79−80
   collaboration, 68−69
   factors motivating faculty to collaborate with librarians, 76−78
   faculty's literature suggestions, 81*f*, 82*f*
   information literacy, 69−70
   librarians embedded in faculty's class instruction, 80−82
   methodology, 70
      interviews, 71−73
      participants, 70−71
      social network analysis, 71
   recommendations for practice, 83−84
Teaching information literacy, integrating ethics in, 31−33. *See also* Information literacy (IL)

Teaching social network, 68
　faculty's, 74–75
　influential elements in, 73–74, 73*f*
Team teaching, 69
TECH 120, 129–130
Technology course, 129–130. *See also*
　　　Communication course
　elements of consultation, 131*t*
　information consulting in, 130–131
　informed learning in, 130, 131*t*
　3.5-hour face-to-face modules, 110
　　designing tutorials/presentations, 111
　　learning theories, 110–111
　　teaching practices, 111
　　and reflection, 111–112
Transfer of learning, 58, 68, 93–94
Transversal skills, 38–39
Twitter, 126–127

## U
University of Auckland, 108
　LLS, 108
　Presenter Training program, 108–109

## V
Victorian Certificate of Education (VCE), 138–139

## W
Wang's curriculum integration model, 113
Whole-school action plan approach, 39–40
Wikipedia, 55

## Z
Zone of proximal development (ZPD), 112

CPSIA information can be obtained
at www.ICGtesting.com
Printed in the USA
FFOW02n1306061017
40813FF